Indo-Asian Geopolitics

Contemporary Perspectives

Indo-Asian Geopolitics

Contemporary Perspectives

Edited by

R Srinivasan

SL Deshmukh

Ashok Kumar Dua

Jayakrishnan N Nair

HOW
ACADEM/CS
an imprint of Highlyy Publishing LLP

in association with

DRaS

PRAGHNA CENTRE FOR RESEARCH. TOWARDS A KNOWLEDGE DRIVEN SOCIETY.
PRAGHNA

ISBN: 978-93-95522-19-9 (Hardbound)
First Published : 2023

Cataloging in Publication Data--DK
Courtesy: D.K. Agencies (P) Ltd. <docinfo@dkagencies.com>
Indo-Asian geopolitics : contemporary perspectives.
pages cm
"This book is the product of 18 months of research by the interns of DRaS-Praghna Research Writing Program which commenced in July 2021"--Acknowledgement.
Includes index.
ISBN 9789395522199
1. Geopolitics--India. 2. Geopolitics--Asia. 3. India--Foreign relations--Asia. 4. Asia--Foreign relations--India. I. Defence Research and Studies (India), issuing body. II. Praghna Centre for Research (Coimbatore, India), issuing body, publisher.
LCC DS450.A78I53 2023 | DDC 954.05 23

Published by : HOW ACADEMICS
an imprint of Highlyy Publishing LLP

Correspondence Address : 4/30 A II Floor, Double Storey Buildings
Vijay Nagar, Delhi-110009
Editorial: +91 9811026449
Sales : +91 9999953412
Email: info@howacademics.com
Website: www.howacademics.com

Printed in India

Foreword

Vice Admiral MP Muralidharan AVSM & Bar, NM (Retd)
Former Director General, Indian Coast Guard

Increasing interdependence between nations and the emergence of Indo Pacific as one geo economic and security zone in the 21st century has given India, with her strategic location in the region, the opportunity to emerge as an influential power in the international arena. Her soft power attributes, adherence to democratic values and principled stands on international issues, give her an advantage that few other countries have. Today many nations in the world are looking at India as a strategic partner to safeguard their interests. Needless to say, knowledge-based approach is essential to succeed in geopolitics and economics. The role played by treatises such as Arthashastra in making ancient Kingdom in India dominant world powers of their era is well known.

The articles contained in this edited book deal with conceptual aspects like multilateralism and national identity. Both these provide the backgrounds to the well-researched articles by DRaS-Praghna interns on India's security concerns owing to the dominant role that China is attempting to play in South Asia. By factoring India's relations with Taiwan, the book attempts to span frontiers that should be of immense interest to students of international relations everywhere.

Against this background, the Research Writing Program jointly initiated by DRaS and Praghna, is a laudable initiative towards steering young students to emerge as scholars of eminence. The programme would go a long way in encouraging the coming generations to carry out in depth study of emerging issues through scientific research and logical analysis. Even more praise worthy is the provision of recognized platforms such as Electronic Journal of Social and Strategic Studies and DRaS Website, where young scholars can publish their findings and observations.

I wish the Founders of DRaS, Praghna and the Mentors of this program all success in their endeavors. It is indeed a much welcome initiative, which has started in a commendable manner, but we have a long way to go before we can rest our oars.

Kochi
09 Jan 2023

Muralidharan MP
Vice Admiral (Retd)

Preface

Scholarship on international relations in India has for long been influenced by theories and constructs that have emanated from other parts of the world. The colonial legacy perhaps has played a key role since India is still being viewed as part of the western thinking, expecting thereby that India will or even should view the world as imagined from a western perspective.

We are aware that colonial India was part of the British Empire's view of the world, and an integral part of the Great game involving the Empire and Czarist Russia. Therefore when independent India embarked upon a foreign policy that rested on principles like Panchsheel and Non-Alignment, it was received with scepticism and suspicion. The ideological battleground of the Cold War actually accentuated the sceptical attitude of the west, precariously pushing India into situations where independent pursuit of foreign policy became a challenge.

However daunting the domestic challenges like poverty, economic stagnation, etc, India managed to stand on its own right during aftermath of the Bay of Pigs Crisis, Chinese aggression, three wars imposed on it by Pakistan and even the eventual disintegration of USSR. The globalization process that commenced in the post-USSR era, presented India with opportunities to rise as an economic power. Earlier, helping Bangladesh emerge as an independent nation had established India's prestige as a potent military power. Coursing on her new found strength, India now has emerged as the 4th largest economy and by scholarly estimates poised to become the 2nd or 3rd largest in about a decade from now.

The global environment in which India is placed now has challenges emanating from its past as well as those that have the potential to rise in future. Principal among these challenges are the rivalry that Pakistan entertains towards India and the seemingly festering Sino-Indian border issues.

Conclusive defeat in conventional war with India has prompted Pakistan to foster and deploy terrorism as a tool against India. Sensing the shift in US priorities post its pull-out from Afghanistan and the ambitions of China to take its BRI dream forward, Pakistan has consciously allied itself with China for what it perceives as a win-win relationship. For China, this amity enables reaching the Arabian Sea through Gwadar Port, cutting its logistics costs by over 50 percent; for Pakistan, it signals perennial supply of weapons, protection at UNSC through China's veto power, and possible economic revival through the 'jewel' of BRI scheme, the China Pakistan Economic Corridor (CPEC). Pakistan's internal dynamics, the excessive hold over its democratic institutions by the fundamentalist clergy and its own Army, however pose questions on Pakistan's ability to be a reliable partner in

CPEC. Oppression of Baluch people and the unrest in its North Western Provinces raise serious challenges to achieving the estimated economic benefits, apart from endemic corruption and apparently self-serving political class in Pakistan.

The rise of Taliban in Afghanistan after the pull-out US troops created a vacuum that Taliban successfully filled. Isolated across the world and branded a terrorist group, Taliban and its Afghanistan are also at crossroads. Stability in Afghanistan has paramount impact in South Asian Region and beyond. Its success could boost the morale of fundamentalist Islamic groups like ISIS and Boko Haram from establishing their own versions of Caliphate; its failure on the other hand, could spill over into terrorist violence in India, Iran, Tajikistan, and China's Xinjiang region. These prospects have compelled regional and extra-regional players to find ways to reach out to Taliban and Afghan people. India's own security matrix is at serious peril if Taliban duly assisted by Pakistan's ISI were to turn their attention to Kashmir.

India's security challenges are not limited to its northern borders or neighbours alone. China's outreach into Bay of Bengal, Arabian Sea and the east coast of Africa accentuate those challenges. With over 55 percent of her trade passing through South China Sea, mitigating challenges through bilateral, multilateral and other avenues with countries in the Indo-pacific region become important. Even though American pressure resulted in reducing her oil imports from Iran in 2019, Indo-Iranian relations continue to be on a strong platform. The Chabahar Port project, though temporarily at a low, appears to be coming back on track. India has also reached out to UAE and Saudi Arabia, taking its relations to a new level through constructive engagement. On the Pacific side of its concerns, India has also enhanced its relations with Taiwan, in addition to its excellent relations with Japan and South Korea. The formation of QUAD has also brought India-Australia-Japan-USA on a framework that has potential to negate the challenges that China could pose to India's interests. Though India has not officially renounced its 'One China Policy', the enhanced cooperation with Taiwan could be critical to balance the power play in the Indo-Pacific Region.

The general context presented above is the foundation on which the articles in this book attempt to discourse individual elements. It must be said that the book attempts to do so in two ways. In the first part it presents two chapters that deal with the concepts of nations, national identity and war, and multilateralism and minilateralism. These conceptual backgrounders are relevant since India's security concerns, especially in the present world order, have to be negotiated with clear conceptual understanding of the formats that drive international relations. In so far as India's security concerns in South Asia, recognizing how the concepts of nationalism and national identity influence the behaviour of nations in the neighbourhood is fundamental to arriving at solutions that will promote its own interests without treading on those of the neighbourhood. To this extent, including three chapters that deal with these aspects lay down the context in which further analysis of India's relations with neighbours and extended neighbourhood is rendered meaningful.

The ten articles presented therefore, deal with the conceptual aspects in the first three chapters, before embarking upon country specific appraisal. A synoptic overview of the articles follows in the succeeding paragraphs.

Understanding the interrelationship between national identity and war is never an easy task. In the case of India and Pakistan the task becomes further daunting. "National Identity and war: The case of India and Pakistan" by K Vikas Sreevatsa helps the readers to comprehend the complexities of the subject at hand. Starting with concepts of Nation, National Identity and War, the paper analyses India and Pakistan rivalry that germinates from their notions of national identity and their manifestation through conflicts. In conclusion, the paper rightly focuses on the abject commonalities between India and Pakistan and ends with a hope that a rightful focus on commonalities between India and Pakistan would usher an era of peace and prosperity for both the nations.

M. Abdul Fatah in his article entitled "From Multilateralism to Minilateralism – A Conceptual Paradigm" succinctly brings out as to how diverse nation-states diplomatically relate to and cooperate with each other. The paper, with the help of appropriate examples, delves deeper into the differences between multilateralism and minilateralism. The former involves features like 'generalized organizing principles', 'indivisibility', and 'diffused reciprocity' whereas the latter is comparatively less formal but more flexible and functional framework with situational interests and shared values. Minilateral forums, however, lack procedural justice and face trust-deficit from non-members. Nation-states due to increasing difficulties in consensus-based resolution of issues are turning towards minilateralism. This, however, does not mean that multilateralism is losing its importance. Both multilateralism and minilateralism will continue to be the subject of future research and play complementary roles depending on the situational issues in wide-ranging geo-political context.

K Vikas Sreevatsa in his article "Nations, National Identity and Nationalism" has illustrated the distinction between the Nation, identity and nationalism. Globalisation of world has left no boundaries between nations with respect to trade, tourism and other economic activates and it has bridged the haves and have nots across the world. Richer nations are now perceiving difficulty due this narrowing disparity. The political leaderships in these nations are now using national identity as a potential tool for political mileage. Many nations have become nationalistic towards protecting the interest of their population. High degree of nationalism among the nations can be a hindrance to development and furtherance of globalisation in coming years. The author clearly demarcates the concepts of nationalism and the relationship with identity. The paper avers that both National identity and Nationalism are to be played out for the benefit of the nations and globalisation.

Rohini Saini in her paper titled "Exploring Pakistan as a Reliable Partner for China and its Implications in India" has focused on China-Pakistan relationship and lucidly brought out importance of the China Pakistan Economic Corridor (CEPC) in relation to China's Belt and Road Initiative (BRI) project. The author has accurately analyzed benefits of CEPC both for China and Pakistan and its economic and security implication for India. The subject has been well researched and has been presented in a logical manner giving cohesive view to the readers. Cogent analysis related to Pakistan's inability to be a reliable partner for China in the long run makes it easier for the readers to understand the complex nuances. In addition, the analysis of China's attempts to encircle India, China's emphasis on faster completion of CPEC, its security implications for India and impact of India's Defence Strategy and Defence Budget is realistic and relevant for the military planners and strategic community. The conclusion is apt, in pointing out the aftermath of failure of Pakistan to fulfil its role in CPEC, the implications for India and some constructive way forward.

The next two articles focus on Afghanistan and implications for India.

Dev Bhatiya in his article entitled "Decoding Taliban and India's Changing Stakes in Afghanistan" discusses the security situation in Afghanistan post US troop withdrawal in 2021 and its implications for India. The paper brings out the significant role played by India in infrastructural development of Afghanistan and its expectations for early completion of the infrastructural projects. The author underscores that "India's role in Taliban-led Afghanistan would be limited and New Delhi may not be able to have the same influence as before." India, therefore, needs to evolve and follow a pragmatic approach towards Taliban-ruled Afghanistan keeping in view the strategic implications for her internal security and economic interests, concludes the author.

In yet another article "Taliban in Afghanistan – India's Security Challenges", Shristi Choudhary, explores the challenges posed by developments in Afghanistan after withdrawal of US-led security forces and options for India. The author highlights that not only India's investment of US Dollar $ 3 billion in various infrastructural projects including Salma Dam are at stake but also, more importantly, the strategic and friendly relationship between the two countries is at peril. Besides, likely rise of terrorism, increasing involvement of Pakistan, and growing influence of China may adversely impact India's security concerns. India, thus, needs to engage constructively but cautiously with Taliban-ruled Afghanistan regime to safeguard her own interests.

The next two articles focus on China and Taiwan.

Anaswara Joy takes a look at One China Principle that remains at the core of China's ambitions to integrate Taiwan into its fold. Steeping beyond the well-known arguments in western scholarship that portrays China's postures on Taiwan as affecting international order and as a threat to democracy, she attempts to understand One China Principle from Chinese point of view. Considering that the United States' proclaimed position on Taiwan, she also evaluates the ambiguities surrounding USA's proclamations and practice. Discoursing on 'One Country Two Systems' approach of China, she finds that US ambiguity lends space for China to continue to exploit it to its advantages. The author then proposes two solutions that could perhaps be considered for resolving the China-Taiwan issue that will bring stability to SCS and the world at large.

Satya Pulukuri has a refreshing view on India's role in his article "India - Taiwan Relations: Should India Continue to Stay Neutral". The author has done a fair research on the current geopolitical developments in Asia pacific region considering the hegemony being enjoyed by China in the region. In view adventurism shown by China in Ladakh and Indian Ocean Region, India should not hesitate to review her relationship with Taiwan. India needs to shift from her current neutral position towards Taiwan and recognise Taiwan as a fully independent nation in the coming years. In nutshell, the author hints that the time has come for India to engage more with Taiwan disregarding the One China Policy (OCP). India should explore the opportunities to replace China with Taiwan in many trade related activities benefiting both India and Taiwan.

The two end chapters are quite unique in their own way, blending into the maze of evolving geopolitical concerns, but pointing to the potentials that the subject of their contents have in making a stable world order.

The world is witnessing a change in the manner in which conflicts are now being conducted. Conventional military conflicts are increasingly giving space to a shadow war that is being conducted through private military contractors (PMC). The PMC that apparently strated as mere support elements are now actively taking part in offensive operations. While this development is perhaps a process of evolution in warfare, unlike standing armies, the PMC remain outside the core principle of accountability. Developed nations are utilizing PMC to further both their politico-economic objectives as well as strategic-tactical objectives too. The Russo-Ukraine conflict that is currently raging has added a mutated dimension to PMC where they are being treated on par with enlisted armies, while still remaining outside accountability for their actions.

Taking again a unconventional approach to strategic affairs, Aman Sharma evaluates the contours of PMC, their role and outreach through case studies. Keeping the international initiatives like ICoC, he attempts to tease the present context in order to bring a framework of accountability to attend on PMC, in his paper titled 'Soldiers for Hire: Contextualising the Private Military's Legal Conundrums'. His paper emphasises the need for international consensus to apportion responsibility on states employing PMC and accountability for their actions, lest nations with vested interests could use PMC for initiating proxy wars while avowedly standing for peace and stability across the world.

Ridipt Singh in his paper on 'Russia, India, and China Alliance – Towards balancing the world order', steps aside from contemporary narratives on each of these countries. Appreciating that each of these countries pursue a political philosophy, governance style and national interests that are distinctly different from each other, he embarks upon the feasibility of their alliance as partners in the emerging world order. Using common currency as a test case, he evaluates the pros and cons, tailoring the challenges in implementing it by such diverse partners, and arrives at the necessity of three of the biggest players in international arena the need to step aside from narrow national interests in order to evolve into a bloc that could bring stability and peace to the world.

Substantial research by each of the contributors and their reliance on primary and secondary sources render their analysis the merit of contemplation.

Praghna Centre for Research (Praghna) and Defence Research and Studies (DRaS) believe that fostering original research and exploring beyond stereotypes is necessary if the society is to become a knowledge driven one. The opinions and deductions arrived at by the contributors are by no means, a judgement or adopted stand on contemporary world affairs. They are driven by a quest for knowledge that arises from research which should guide further impartial analyses on world affairs.

Both Praghna and DRaS do hope that these objectives will be met by scores of young researchers who could take the cue from the contents of this book.

Gp Capt R Srinivasan VSM (Retd)

Editors' Note

Praghna Centre for Research (Praghna) and Defence Research and Studies (DRaS) collaborated to formulate a research methodology and writing internship for students who are keen to acquire the knowledge and refine their skill at undertaking scientific research into social and strategic studies.

DRaS-Praghna Research Writing Program is now one year old. As mentors in the program and Editors of this Volume, we note the quality of the research works contained herein with satisfaction.

The initiative of these two institutions culminated in the publication of eight research works (three research papers, one book review and four research articles). Encouraged by the enthusiasm and ability of young researchers, Praghna and DRaS have taken one more step in bringing out this Volume of research by their Interns that includes ten papers.

The objective is to make the previously published electronic content in a print book form that could serve as reference material for other researchers and libraries. Through this initiative, both Praghna and DRaS intend to foster a scientific quest for substantive research in social and strategic studies.

The mentorship by the editors has been a journey of exploration of new thoughts, intense debate and combined with great learning for all. By bringing out this biook, we intend to take the quest for substantial research in social and strategic studies to newer frontiers.

We acknowledge the untiring efforts by our mentees and wish them the best in all their research endeavours.

09 Dec 2022

GpCapt (Dr) R Srinivasan VSM (Retd)

Cmde SL Deshmukh NM (Retd)

Cdr (Prof) (Dr) AK Dua (Retd)

Cdr JK Nair (Retd)

About the Editors

Group Captain R Srinivasan VSM (Retd), PhD is Editor-in-Chief of Electronic Journal of Social and Strategic Studies, an online research journal. He is also the Founder-Director of Praghna Centre for Research. He is a freelancing academician and a Scopus indexed author with over 13 book chapters on governance, Environmental social movements, human rights and political economy published internationally. He has published over 30 research articles through eminent Think Tanks on International affairs. He retired as Group Captain from Indian Air Force with over three decades of service, in 2018. He was awarded Visisht Seva Medal for distinguished service to the country, by Hon'ble President of India in 2012. He holds a PhD in Political Sociology, apart from an MSW, LL B and PG Diploma in International Humanitarian Law. He mentors emerging scholars on research writing.

Commodore SL Deshmukh NM (Retd), has served in the Indian Navy for 32 years. His educational qualifications include BE (Mech), MSc (DefSc), PGDM (Gold Medallist). He holds a qualification both in Marine & Aviation fields. He served on-board ships & Aircraft carriers. He is specialist on the maintenance of Fighter aircraft and Anti Submarines Warfare Helicopters. He held many operational and administrative appointments including Principal Director at Naval HQ, Commodore Superintendent Naval Aircraft Yard, Director Naval Institute of Aeronautical Technology and Project Director of a major Naval Aviation Project. He is alumni of Defence Services Staff College (Wellington, Nilgiris). Post-retirement from Indian Navy he worked with Tata Group for 5 years and is currently working with SUN Group's Aerospace & Defence vertical (at Gurgaon) as Senior Vice President. He has presented papers at various International Seminars. He is Life Member of Aeronautical Society of India. He also works in the educational field in his spare time. He is an avid writer and writes on Technical matters & issues of common interest. His research papers and articles have been published by C3S India Chennai, DRaS and EJSSS.

Commander (Prof) (Dr) Ashok Dua (Retd) is a naval veteran and an educationist. During his service of over three decades in the Indian Navy, he has held several key appointments, both afloat and ashore, including deputations abroad. He is an alumnus of Defence Services Staff College, Wellington. After retirement from the Indian Navy, he served as Associate Professor at Krishna Institute of Engineering & Technology, Ghaziabad for almost a decade. He obtained his PhD in the area of Ethical Leadership from Aligarh Muslim University. An accredited management teacher of AIMA, he is also FIE, FIETE, MIMA, and LMISTE. He is a volunteer member of Baal Vikaas Bhaaratee and helps inculcate Universal Human Values among young and impressionable school children. He runs a blog http://mpower360.wordpress.com to empower young minds. Currently, as a Senior Fellow of Defence Research and Studies, he is associated with DRaS – Praghna Internship Program helping budding researchers develop their research skills.

Commander (Dr) Jayakrishnan N Nair (Retd, Indian Navy), leading consultant in Defence, Aerospace and Maritime. He is an electronics engineer by profession and specialised in avionics and aerospace systems. He has served the Indian Navy for 25 years and was responsible for successful planning, execution and delivery of several projects and assignments across diverse segments. Key strategist responsible for several turnkey projects and innovations while in service. He is a Fellow of Institution of Engineers, Kolkata. He is a life member of Aeronautical Society of India, All India Management Association, the Computer Society of India and Indian Society of Training and Development. Apart from an MTech (Aerospace) and MBA, he has been honoured with a Doctorate in Advanced Studies (Science) by the University of Azteca, Mexico. He is TDF-DRDO Expert on indigenisation. He is an Associate Member at MP-Institute of Defence Studies and Analyses, New Delhi and Senior Fellow (Defence and Military Analysis) at the Centre for Public Policy Research. He is the Founder and CEO of Defence and Research and Studies and was Senior Advisor to Deloitte Touche Tohmatsu India LLP on Defence Projects. He is an Adjunct Professor at SASTRA University. Currently his work is focused on emerging technologies in defence.

Acknowledgment

This book is the product of 18 months of research by the Interns of DRaS-Praghna Research Writing Program which commenced in July 2021. Promoting scientific quest among students and emerging scholars is the sole objective of the program.

We would like to acknowledge Vice Admiral MP Muralidharan, AVSM & Bar, NM (Retd), former Director General of Indian Coast Guard, who graciously agreed to read through, appreciate and provide the Foreword for this volume.

We also acknowledge the deep sense of purpose and support that Praghna Centre for Research (Praghna) and Defence Research and Studies (DRaS) provided to conduct the program the end result of which is this book, that speaks for itself.

Commodore SL Deshmukh NM (Retd), Commander (Prof) (Dr) AK Dua (Retd), Ph.D., Commander JK Nair (Retd), Founder-Director of DRaS have been the pillars of this program and their cooperation, commitment and enthusiasm to bring this volume is deeply appreciated.

We are happy to acknowledge the enthusiasm with which the interns committed themselves to learn and produce these ten articles that bear testimony to their conceptual and research abilities.

HOW Academics, in particular, Mr. Kanav Kansra's enthusiasm is infectious. As our publisher, the team at How Academics have walked every step of the way, bringing this book to its present form and its publication in a delightfully smooth manner.

Coimbatore — Dr R Srinivasan

Contents

1. National Identity and War: The case of India and Pakistan

K Vikas Sreevatsa[1]

Abstract

The paper attempts to study the interrelation of war and national identity. It will establish a theoretical framework for nations, nationalism, national identity and the impact of national identity on war and vice versa. Wars start as a clash of national identities, and the longer it perpetuates it gets absorbed into the identity discourse. Hence, as wars stretch longer, the chances of arbitration grow narrower as nations start identifying the war with their nationhood. The paper further analyses the Indo-Pak conflict within the frame work of clash of national identities. It focuses on demarcating India and Pakistan's national identity and studies the conflict. It concludes that to arbitrate a conflict between nations a historical analysis of the nations in question and a grass roots ethnographic research of war narratives is pertinent.

Keywords: National Identity, War, India, Pakistan, Kashmir, Nations, Indo-Pak Conflict

Introduction

Fascination with war and its multiple facets continues to intrigue scholars around the world. Homer, Thucydides to modern day Tolstoy have written about war. Earlier wars were fought between kingdoms and empires, modern day wars, apart from instances of unconventional war by non-state actors, are fought between nations. Hence, it is pertinent to inquire into nations.

Each nation has identifiers that help bind the nation into a solidarity. These identifiers are dynamic and define the nation at a particular space and time. The survival of any national arrangement depends on the intensity to which the nation identifies with their national identity. This makes national identity an important

1 K Vikas Sreevatsa is a Masters student in Global Studies from B.R. Ambedkar University, Delhi

subject of analyses when discussing war. The paper attempts to analyze how national identity and war impact each other. It will further dwell into the Indo-Pak conflict which continues to perpetuate in the 21st Century. If not hot war, there is a perpetual situation of hot peace between India and Pakistan. Kashmir remains one of the most heavily militarized zones in the world. Hence, on the basis of a theoretical framework, the paper will attempt to study the Indo-Pak conflict and endeavor to understand the deadlock in arbitration with a look at their respective national identities

The paper is divided into two sections. The first section will begin by defining national identity. To define national identity an inquiry into nations and nationalism is pertinent. My previous research on nations, nationalism and national identity (Sreevatsa, 2022) will be borrowed to form a conceptual framework. It will further attempt to form a frame work of the impact of national identity on war and vice versa. The second section will proceed to define Indian national identity and Pakistani national identity, before diving into the Indo-Pak conflict and its relation with their national identities. Indo-Pak conflict is of particular importance, as these nations sprung out of a bloody partition and a future potential border conflict that perpetuates to this day. Their post-independence identity is overpowered by the conflict.

I

What is a Nation?

Hugh Seton-Watson (Seton-Watson, 1977) attempts to define a Nation, "Nation is a community of people, whose members are bound by a sense of solidarity". A nation exists when, not all, but a significant number of people in a community consider themselves to form a nation. By virtue of this definition, even social groups based on ethnicity, linguistics, religion come under the ambit of a nation. These social group are also bound by a sense of solidarity and consider themselves as a collective. On the other end of the spectrum, Stalin in his work "Marxism and the National question" (Stalin, 1913) believes,

> A nation is a historically constituted, stable community of people, formed on the basis of a common language, territory, economic life, and psychological make-up manifested in a common culture

But as Stalin asserts, all the elements namely history, community, language, territory, economy, psychology, are a prerequisite to a nation. He states, "It is sufficient for a single one of these characteristics to be lacking and the nation ceases to be a nation". This definition of nation by nature is overtly rigid for the contemporary multicultural world. By virtue of this definition, most of modern day nations would cease to qualify as nations. For Benedict Anderson, (Anderson, 1983), a nation "is an imagined political community – and imagined as both inherently limited and sovereign". Imagined because members of even the smallest nation have no ways of interacting with every other member but are still united under the communion of the nation. Limited as even the largest nations are finite in their territory beyond which lie other nations, and do not imagine themselves "co-terminus with mankind".

Understanding the distinction between Hugh Seton-Watson's approach to defining a nation, and Anderson's definition of nation is crucial. Seton-Watson's definition better exemplifies a social group. Any group of people, who share a vision of commonality are a social group. According to Omar Dahbour (Dahbour, 2002), group identity is the social seed that forms the foundation of the idea of a nation. These social groups could be associated based on ethnicity, linguistics, religion, history, culture, etc. A nation adheres to Anderson definition, of an imagined communion which recognises its right to self-determination (sovereignty) in a specific territorially demarcated space. Not all social groups are sovereign or recognise their right to self-determination. Modern day multi-cultural nation-states, may constitute under them, numerous social groups, under the overall communion of a nation. In a nation, none of the social groups are sovereign, but their communion, the nation, is sovereign. Dissatisfaction with the national arrangement might lead social groups to recognise their right to self-determination, and hence form a separate nation by way of succession movements.

Nationalism

Nationalism has dual existence, as it precedes and proceeds the nation. It manifests during the national struggle, as a means of social mobilization for the national cause, to realize their rights of self-determination, and during the post-independence period to consolidate the nation. Hence, A. D. Smith (Smith A. , 1983) defines nationalism as,

> An ideological movement for the attainment and maintenance of self-government and independence on behalf of a group, some of whose members conceive it to constitute an actual or potential 'nation'

The symbols used to invigorate nationalism could be cultural, linguistic, historical, etc. War and sacrifice are also used as emblems of nationalism. These symbols contribute to the molding of the national identity. Pre- independence nationalism concerns itself with first, delimiting the aspects of the aspiring nation with respect to people as well as territory, second, in empowering the citizenry to their right to self-determination.

Nationalism plays a crucial role in the post-independence consolidation process. But the distinction lies in that nationalism after the formation of the nation is state directed. Han Kohn's definition of nationalism (Kohn, n.d.) better describes post-independence nationalism, as an "ideology based on the premise that the individual's loyalty and devotion to the nation-state surpass other individual or group interests". Post-Independence Nationalism is a virtue of loyalty to the nation. Hence nationalism, post-independence, is directed towards eroding traditional group loyalties and prescribing to national loyalties. Smith (Smith A. D., 1971) in his work details the aspiration of post-independence nationalism as integrating the nationals into a homogenous unit.

Understanding National Identity

Most nations have under their ambit multiple social groups. Narratives, real or imaginary, have to be construed to give these various social groups, direct stakes, in relation to the nation. These narratives could be drawn historically, culturally, linguistically, religiously, ethnographically, etc. aiding the construction of the National Identity. National Identity can be viewed as an abstract ideologue, dynamic in nature that unites different people of different social groups into an imagined communion of a nation. In diverse societies, constructing a national identity connecting all the diverse social groups to the nation, is a challenging endeavor. In these societies, national identity takes the form of moral values and codes that are humanist in nature. Ideas such as pluralism, secularism, democracy, equality, liberty come under the moral doctrines that bind social groups to the nation. To redeem their right to self-determination, the nation forms a state. The project of nation building involves the state constructing narratives that unites the social groups under the communion of the nation.

National identity is dynamic in nature and changes with time. The changes to the national identity might not be uniformly assimilated across social groups which may lead to frictions. When these changes fall outside the purview of comprehension of social groups, the nation as an entity becomes unstable. The role of the state is the keep track of the changing tides of national identity and constantly construct inclusive narratives.

War and National Identity

The idea of a self-determination is intrinsic to the idea of a nation. When two or more nation's actions, or interests coincide, a conflict is inevitable. When conflict persists, tensions among nations intensify, which may lead them to go to war. King Gundobald believes war to be an international trail. He states (Park, 1941),

Between civilized nations also war is the form of litigation by which states make their claims valid.

By-product of war, irrespective of the results, is death, destruction and suffering. The nation as a whole, celebrates, grieves and processes the war together which forms the basis of collective memory. Paul M.M Doolan (Doolan, 2021) studies this collective memory. He states,

Collective memory contains no essence, no immutable status or transcendental being. It does not exist in some ethereal sphere waiting to be discovered. Instead, it is a mediated memory that, as Jan Assman suggests, is "stored away in symbolic form".

Contextualising collective memory to the nation, Amos Funkenstein (Funkenstein, 1989) states,

> Nations are meant to remember their heroes "forever"; to perpetuate the memory of a person means to embed it in the collective memory

The state attempts to transform this collective memory into a national identifier by way of museums, national holidays, etc.

Nation-states primary role is protecting the nation's right to self-determination, with disregard towards others self-interests. Conflicts mobilize the nation and hence is a trial by fire for any nation, representing a test of the strength of their conviction. War is the product of a clash of national identities and with time molds each respective national identity. Samuel Huntington (Huntington, 1996) in his work 'Clash of Civilizations' hypothesis the existence of seven, possibly eight civilizations categorized culturally. He predicts future conflicts as a clash among these civilizations. He states:

> Nation states are and will remain the most important actors in world affairs, but their interests, associations, and conflicts are increasingly shaped by cultural and civilizational factors.

Huntington emphasis on the identity aspects of international conflicts.

National identity being abstract requires an element of tangibility to proliferate and be considered credible. War as an event brings tangibility to the imagined communion, eventually evolving into a testimony of national identity. War becomes part of the collective memory of the nation and gives a sense of a shared national experience. Victories in war form part of national pride, giving credence to the national identity over others. Loss in war and the human cost of war provides a new life to the nation in search of purpose for their loss. Martyrs become immortal heroes to be looked upon to find national strength and unity. Ernest Renan believes the nation itself to be defined by its past escapades, victories and losses. He believes national unity is directly related to the national suffering a nation has endured, and regards past glories to be the best social asset. To Renan (Renan, 1990),

> A nation is a large-scale solidarity, constituted by the feeling of sacrifices that one has made in the past, and of those one is prepared to make in the future.

Renan hence, emphasises the importance of the human cost of war in influencing national identity narratives.

During a war, the nation as a whole is mobilised. National loyalties supersede regional loyalties. In case of a loss, the nation may choose, as a defensive strategy, to blame certain social groups for the loss, to protect the integrity and respect for the nation as a whole. An example of this is post-World War 1 Germany, where the loss of World War 1 was blamed disproportionately on the Jews. Hence, war acts as a great unifier or as an impetus to the eventual breakup of the national arrangement. The importance of national identity in any conflict is clearly postulated by Gareth Evans (Evans, 2011),

> The sense of national identity is never stronger than when countries are at war with each other, at imminent risk of war, or remembering war…….it is war, the prospect of war, and the memory of war that has traditionally shaped and defined that collective national sentiment and sense-of-self we think of as being at the core of national identity. By defending oneself, the nation demarcates the "other" and in the process defines itself more concretely.

Wars fought by nations become part of their national identity. The room for arbitration of disputes in the case of ongoing wars grows narrower as nations are sceptical about negotiating with their national identifiers. In this way, negotiations in war threatens the nation as it dilutes their respective national identity. This is more prominent in the case of the losing side since any compromise is seen as a betrayal to the fallen men. Wars have a tendency to perpetuate, to give meaning to the sacrifices of the fallen, and in the hope of avenging them with undisputed victory. The winning side attach a sense of pride with the war further alienating any form of negotiation. Hence, war and it becoming a national identifier, provides the war with a life of its own, perpetuating in continuity. Compromises can be observed when the nations stop valuing the loss, either in the fear of further suffering or because they evolve away from the premise of the conflict.

II

The Case of India and Pakistan

The Indo-Pak conflict is one of the enduring legacies of British Imperialism in the Indian Sub-continent. It is the direct result of the divide and rule policy adopted by the British. The deliberate state action to divide a diverse India under communal lines led to the horrors of the partition. Since independence, India and Pakistan have fought four major wars. Post the Kargil conflict, which saw the world edge dramatically close to a nuclear confrontation, Pakistan has ventured into unconventional warfare. According to Ministry of Home Affairs, (Ministry of Home Affairs, GoI, 2005) Pakistan:

> has recruited, trained, financed, armed and Infiltrated terrorist in India...... Pakistan has not yet dismantled the terrorism infrastructure in the territory under its control. This infrastructure is continued to be sponsored and used by Pak-ISI to recruit, train and finance terrorists and infiltrate them into India.

As of 2022, Pakistan has been retained in the Financial Action Task Force (FATF) Grey List, and has been scrutinized for its role in terrorist financing, money laundering and proliferation financing.

The rest of the paper will analyse the national identities of India and Pakistan. It will delve into the impact of the Indo-Pak conflict on their respective identities.

Indian National identity

A recognition of the diversity of the Indian nation is critical to understand the complexity of Indian national identity. India is an enigma for social scientist. India represents 17.7% of the world population. It has 23 official languages. It is multi-ethnic and multi-cultural. Nationhood based on language, ethnicity, culture fall short of explaining Indian nationhood. Shashi Tharoor (Tharoor, From Midnight to Millennium, 1997) states:

India embraces the extraordinary mixture of ethnic groups, the profusion of mutually incomprehensible languages, the varieties of topography and climate, the diversity of religions and cultural practices, and the range of levels of economic development.

But, a narrative, constructs an identity that binds this incomprehensible diversity under a single communion. Indian national identity is a product of the interdependence model of nation building as contrast to the integrative model (Gautam, 1985). This model envisioned an interdependence among the diversity.

> .... national culture is conceived in composite terms. Culture is associated with land and its people and not with religion. Indian nationalist intellectuals conceived Indian culture as a composite culture in the making of which all religious and social group have made their contribution over time. (Gautam, 1985)

Hence, in the case of India, the definition of nation, has to be altered to, a multi-ethnic community in which different ethnic groups while retaining their ethnic identity resolve any conflict between national and ethnic identities in favour of the nation. (Gautam, 1985)

India held a centre stage in world trade and pilgrimage through history. This brought India in contact with diverse people and cultures. The Indian subcontinent has been invaded from the north numerous times by central Asian khanates, as well as by the Greek. Culturally, India rarely remained static. Any culture or religion that entered India, was envisioned to have moulded Indian culture, as they were moulded by Indian culture, metamorphosing a unique Indian variant. Recognising Paul Gilroy's (Gilroy, 1995) "melting pot" metaphor, he states,

> National identity.... subordinates ethnic, racial, religious and cultural differences to the assimilating logic of a common culture, or the 'melting pot'

Indian nation is better described by, as Shashi Tharoor (Tharoor, What is India?, 2018) states, the "thali" metaphor. Shovana Ray (Ray, 2017) states, "Centuries of Indian civilization and years of amalgamation of various traditions, mould today's Indian citizen". This aspect of the diversity of India forms the bedrock of commonality. The different practices and nuances of culture that are articulated in India are unique to the geography of the Indian subcontinent. Shoyana Ray states, "With all evident diversities, Indians share common components, like, way of life, values, norms, etc."

Among Miller's (Miller, 1995) axioms of nationality, the belief in the existence of a national community and historical continuity stand out in the case of India. The existence of a national community was realised as a product of the national struggle during colonial times. The struggle for Independence bound different groups under a single communion to attain independence and sovereignty. The Indian National Congress, which spear headed the Indian independence movement, focussed on creating narratives that were universally inclusive to bind the nation together. Historical continuity was drawn from the time of the Indus Valley civilisation to colonial times, in a civilizational sense. The unit of continuity, in traditional cases being language, lineage, etc., in India's case, was seen as the whole unit of the Indian geography, which is east of the river Indus. The Indian national movement, constructed inclusive national identifiers as a tool of social mobilisation for the national cause and used a historic perspective and a common struggle to bind the diversity under a commonality. Hence, India realised its civilizational existence and achieved national conscience.

Indian identity adopted humanist moral doctrines to bridge the diversity of norms and cultures. Doctrines such as liberty, equality, fraternity, justice, secularism were adopted as identifying markers as evident from the preamble of the Indian constitution (GOI, n.d.). These ideals are revered across cultures, bridging the gaps between them. To illustrate, the doctrine of equality can be found in the Vedas (considered the bedrock of Hinduism):

The Vedas speak highly of equality and brotherhood... "The entire world is a family" was the motto of Vedic civilization. All had equal opportunity in all walks of life in Vedic civilization. (Pandey, 2014)

Similar doctrine can be found Buddhism which preaches, 'According to Buddhism, equality is not fragmentary and sectional, but complete and universal.' (Biu, 2003). In Islam

> ...God has given man this right of equality as a birth right. Therefore, no man should be discriminated against on the ground of the colour of his skin, his place of birth, the race or the nation in which he was born. ('Ala Maudoodi, Ahmad, & Khan, 1976)

Adopting the Right to Equality under Article 14 of the Indian Constitution, helps bridge the other differences that arises among Hinduism, Buddhism and Islam by enshrining the equality of all human beings.

Indian national identity is a product of moral doctrines, history of diversity and a process of cultural amalgamation. Constitution of any nation is a document laminating the past and envisioning the future. India derives and laminates its identifiers in its preamble. All these fragmented identifiers are perfectly articulated by the phrase, "Unity in Diversity". This provides the tolerant, inclusive doctrine that Indians idealise as an identifier.

Pakistani National Identity

The nation of Pakistan being a part of the Indian sub-continent has shared a common history. While defining their nationhood and national identity, Pakistan had to make a conscious effort to differentiate itself from India. During the colonial struggle, the demand for an Islamic nationhood was under the overall struggle for sovereignty and independence from the imperial. At the dawn of Independence, with the proclamation of partition, Pakistan had a megalith task of defining and differentiating its nationality.

The fear of the Muslim community, being suppressed in a democratic, Hindu-majority nation, led to formulating a two-nation theory. The two-nation theory was antithetical to India's view of a melting pot culture, where each culture that enters India, changes the existing cultures and gets itself changed in the process. The two-nation theory proposed the existence of two distinct nations in the Indian sub-continent, each with its own values and traditions, isolated, and rarely intermingling. Muhammad Ali Jinnah in his presidential address to the Muslim League (Jinnah, Presidential Address to Muslim League, 1940) states,

> The Hindus and Muslims belong to two different religious philosophies, social

> customs, and literature[s]. They neither intermarry nor interdine together, and indeed they belong to two different civilisations which are based mainly on conflicting ideas and conceptions.

Isthiaq Ahmed (Ahmed, 2008) charts Pakistani National identity from the eve of Independence. A commonality based on Islam was constructed, to create a nation which recognizes its right to self-determination. By nature, the Muslim Leagues narrative of nationhood were exclusionary rather than inclusive. But, in the Indian sub-continent, Islam, under its ambit hosts tremendous diversity. During the national struggle, Islam become a social mobiliser for people from Punjab to Bengal. Once independence was realized, the newly formed Pakistan, had to devise methods that shifts loyalty from Islam to Pakistan.

What did the Nation of Pakistan Represent During the National Movement?

300 years prior to the British raj, India was controlled by a series of Muslim dynasties. After the revolt of 1857 and Bahadur Shah II being banished to Burma, the power dynamics changed. The Indian Muslims suddenly realized their minority status. As the INC channeled the national movement with a promise of a democratic independent India, Indian Muslims feared being suppressed by the majority Hindu nation (Kiss, 2013).

The Indian National Congress senior leaders were openly leaning towards socialism as a means to organize the economy upon independence. This made a lobby of landed aristocrats from Punjab and Bengal, who supported the Muslim League's cause for a separate nation, as ways to retain their capital, and in effect their hierarchical supremacy.

There was a network of Muslim clergies, fundamentalist and revivalist who believed, the creation of Pakistan as a nation for Muslims, would preserve the sharia law and the Islamic way of life. Secularism propounded by INC leaders such as M.K. Gandhi and Jawaharlal Nehru was seen as a threat to Islam. This group would later come to play a dominating role in shaping and controlling Pakistani national identity and politics. It is important to mention the lack of unity among this network, with some ullemas and maulvis opposing the demand for Pakistan.

Post-Independence

Muhammad Ali Jinnah attempted to subdue Islam as the identifier post-independence, and envisioned a secular and liberal nation-state. He states (Jinnah, First Presidential Address to the Constituent Assembly of Pakistan, 1947),

> You may belong to any religion or caste or creed that has nothing to do with the

> business of the state. [...] We are starting with this fundamental principle that we are all citizens and equal citizens of one state [...]. Now I think we should keep that in front of us as our ideal and you will find that in course of time Hindus would cease to be Hindus and Muslims would cease to be Muslims, not in the religious sense, because that is the personal faith of each individual, but the political sense as citizens of the state.

Arshi Saleem Hashmi (Hashmi, 2009) states,

> Despite being an Islamic Republic constitutionally, there was a clear division between politics and religion, as well as a distinction between private and public Islam, at least in the formidable years after the creation of Pakistan. Mohammad Ali Jinnah, the founder of Pakistan, in his inaugural address to the Pakistan Constituent Assembly on 11 August 1947, clearly stated that religion was a private affair of the individual and highlighted the equality of religions.

Christopher Jaffrelot (Jaffrelot, 2012) analyses Pakistan's post-independent attempt at secularization. He highlights the inclusion of minority rights in the first two drafts of Pakistan's constitution.

> ...the first two Constitutions of Pakistan did not define Islam as an official religion and recognized important rights to the minorities

But once Islam as a unifier had been established, it resisted any attempt at a change in the discourse. As India celebrated liberty and secularism, Pakistan, to own up to its national claim, was forced to embrace Islam as its moral doctrine. Under Islam, the Ahmediyas has been cast as non-Muslims. (Ahmed, 2008). To homogenise East Pakistan and West Pakistan (the centre of power), Urdu was promoted as the official language. This led to frictions in East Pakistan, where linguistic identity of Bengali, which represented more than just a language but also a continuity of culture, proved to more decisive than their Islamic identity. This led to the Bangladeshi Liberation War of 1971, and the creation of the nation of Bangladesh.

Post liberation of Bangladesh, Pakistan started a process termed as "Islamization' to consolidate power, in the fear of further succession. Riaz Hassan (Hassan, 1985) highlights the process of Islamization of Pakistani society, making it a central aspect of Pakistani national identity. Any confusion with regards to official state policy being inclined towards Islamic ideology or being aspirational towards a secular state was settled during the period of President Zia ul Haq reign.

The Soviet invasion of Afghanistan, and the inherent cold war dynamics, saw USA use Pakistan as a base to counter soviet influence. Again Islam was preached as a social mobiliser against soviet communism. This Islam was more fundamental and rigid in nature. This further empowered the fundamental segments of Pakistani society on their righteousness.

Pakistani National identity, as it evolved through time, is still reflective of Islamic morality. Hence, religion forms the predominant identifier and continues to mobilise society.

Indo-Pak Conflict

Kashmir is the central battlefield of the Indo-Pak conflict. This section will analyse the Indo-Pak conflict with Kashmir at its centre. The genesis of the Indo-Pak conflict lies in their respective narratives of nationhood. As Sumit Ganguly (Ganguly, 1995) states,

> ...can be traced to the profoundly divergent conceptions of nation building that underlie the Indian and Pakistani nationalist movement.............. possession of Kashmir, a Muslim-majority state abutting the two nascent states, consequently assumed a significance far greater than a mere territorial claim

Kashmir for India, represents the essence of Indian secularism. It is symbolic of the Indian experiment, where diversity can co-exist in a federal arrangement, and can shine in the global stage. Kashmir for Pakistan, represents the very essence of its nationhood, the belief in Muslim majority states of South Asia to collectivise under the banner of Islam and protect the Islamic way of life and its purity. As Ambassador V. K. Grover (Grover, 2001) states,

> Pakistan was a creation of the two-nation theory. The same was reduced to ashes when East Pakistan broke away from its western half. Kashmir remains the last fig of the failed two-nation theory........ Pakistan as an entity cannot give up the Kashmir issue if it is to survive.

Hence, the battlefield is not merely India and Pakistan but secularism and communalism. This aspect of the conflict prevents any form of compromise from either states, in the fear of poking holes in their national narratives.

Another dimension to the lack of conflict resolution can be explained through the sunk-cost fallacy in war. Sunk-cost fallacy is the tendency of agents to continue investing money, men and resources in an endeavour, even after continued disappointments and failures, so the initial investment doesn't seem wasteful. If the conflict remains hot, losses aren't eternal and there is a possibility of retribution. Pakistan still holds narratives of a grand victory against India in the future to rationalise the conflict. This can be seen by the comments of Pakistan's Interior Minister, Sheikh Rasdeed Ahmad, on Pakistani Cricket team winning against India as "victory of Islam" (Shams, 2021).

India and Pakistan as nations had their genesis during the partition. Since the partition, India and Pakistan have been at perpetual war, at times hot and at times cold. Hence, the national identity so developed of the respective nations, have been influenced to a great extent by the ongoing conflict, where part of what mobilizes each nation is tensions with the other. Hence, any attempt at arbitration and resolution should take into account the national identity component of the conflict.

Conclusion

The paper started by establishing a theoretical framework of nations, nationalism and national identity. It further ventured into the relation between national identity and war and in this way attempted to study the identity aspect of wars. Is war an independent event or is it intrinsically related to the nation? Viewing wars from a strategic lens or going by state narratives for the war does not comprehensively justify the perpetuation of war. The reasons for continuity of hostility are linked to national identities. War starts and perpetuates as a clash of identities. Any measure of conflict resolution has to take into account the national identifier of the respective state into account. The paper believes any resolution that vows to address a particular conflict without due attention to the underlying identifiers is only a temporary ease of tensions, with the potential to relapse into war in the future. Hence, a study of history of parties to the conflict that evolves from a ground level ethnographic research on war narratives is necessary for concrete solution to end the cause for wars.

The paper took to studying the Indo-Pak conflict through the lens of national identity and found that for both nations, the Kashmir issue represents a test of their national grit. It represents the premise of their respective concept of nationhood. It represents an opportunity for Pakistan to redeem its perceived failures. To India, it represents military glory and the collective strength of the Indian nation against insurmountable odds challenging its sovereign integrity. It therefore follows that any arbitration has to carefully negotiate what Kashmir represents to each nation. Solution to the issue have to manoeuvre through the identifiers to arrive at a compromise where neither India nor Pakistan feel the sense of defeat.

The nations of India and Pakistan have more similarities than they have differences. There are similarities in culture, language, religion, history, etc. Although no formal trade agreement exists, India and Pakistan have an informal trade amounting to USD 4.71 Billion (Taneja & Bimal, 2016). Focusing and building on such similarities and common interests will ameliorate built-up tensions and help dilute the aggressive war narratives prevalent in each nation. The Indian film industry, especially Bollywood, enjoys a tremendous appeal in Pakistan. Sufi music from Pakistan similarly enjoys enormous patronage in India. These factors indicate ample room for cultural diplomacy as means of reconciliation. If both nations chose to focus on their similarities rather than their differences, India and Pakistan can work towards a more peaceful future.

References

Ahmed, I. (2008). *Pakistani National Identity* (1 ed., Vol. 34). Inernational Review of Modern Sociology. Retrieved May 3, 2022, from http://www.jstor.org/stable/41421657

Ala Maudoodi, S. A., Ahmad, K., & Khan, A. S. (1976). Human Rights in Islam. *Allamah Abu al-'A'la Mawdudi al Tawhid Journal, 4*(3). Retrieved May 02, 2022, from https://www.iium.edu.my/deed/articles/hr/hr.html

Anderson, B. (1983). Introduction. In *Imagined Communities : Reflections on the Origin and Spread of Nationalism* (p. 6). London: Verso. Retrieved January 10, 2022, from https://is.muni.cz/el/1423/jaro2016/SOC757/um/61816961/Benedict_Anderson_Imagined_Communities.pdf

Biu, W. C. (2003). The Buddhist Theory of Equality. In W. C. Biu, *The Sceintific Outlook of Buddhism.* Hongkong: Astros Printing Limited. Retrieved March 28, 2022, from https://www.wisdomlib.org/buddhism/essay/the-scientific-outlook-of-buddhism/d/doc2238.html

Dahbour, O. (2002). National Identity : An argument for the Strict Definition. *Public Affairs Quarterly, 16*(1), 17-37. Retrieved April 3, 2022, from http://www.jstor.org/stable/40441311

Doolan, P. M. (2021). Collective Memory and the Dutch East Indies. In P. M. Doolan, *Unremembering Decolonization.* Amsterdam University Press. Retrieved April 11, 2022, from https://doi.org/10.2307/j.ctv209xng5

Evans, G. (2011). War , Peace and National Identity. *Melbourne Festival of Ideas, Sydney Myer Asia Centre.* Retrieved January 13, 2022, from http://www.gevans.org/speeches/speech440.html

Funkenstein, A. (1989). Collective Memory and Histroical Consciousness. *History and Memory, 1*(1), 5-26. Retrieved April 11, 2022, from http://www.jstor.org/stable/25618571

Ganguly, S. (1995). Wars Without End : The Indo-Pak Conflict. *The Annals of the American Acadamy of Political and Social Science, 541*, 167-178. Retrieved April 27, 2022, from http://www.jstor.org/stable/1048283

Gautam, O. P. (1985). The Indian National Congress and Nation Building. *The Indian Journal of Political Science, 46*(4), 487-505. Retrieved April 11, 2022, from http://www.jstor.org/stable/41855201

Gilroy, P. (1995). *The Black Atlantic : Modernity and Double Consciousness.* Harvard University Press. Retrieved April 13, 2022, from https://dl1.cuni.cz/pluginfile.php/756417/mod_resource/content/1/Gilroy%20Black%20Atlantic.pdf

Gilroy, Paul;. (1993). *The Black Atlantic :Modernity and Double Consciousness.* Cambridge: Harvard University Press.

GOI. (n.d.). *Department of Justice*. Retrieved from https://doj.gov.in/sites/default/files/preamble-eng.pdf

Grover, V. (2001, April-June). Appraisal of Indo-Pak Relations. *India Quaterly, 57*(2), 11-16. Retrieved April 27, 2022, from http://www.jstor.org/stable/45073256

Hashmi, A. S. (2009). *Extremism in Pakistan : A brief History.* Institute of Peace and Conflict Studies. Retrieved May 2, 2022, from https://www.jstor.org/stable/resrep33600.4

Hassan, R. (1985). Islamization: An Analysis of Religious, Political and Social Change in Pakistan. *Middle Eastern Studies, 21*(3), 263-284. Retrieved April 2, 2022, from http://www.jstor.org/stable/4283071

Huntington, S. P. (1996). *The Clash of Civilisation and the Remaking of World Order.* New York: Simon Schuster.

Jaffrelot, C. (2012). Secularization without Secularism in Pakistan. *Paris Institute of Political Studies, Sciences Po.* Retrieved January 11, 2022, from https://papers.ssrn.com: https://papers.ssrn.com/sol3/papers.cfm?abstract_id=2282491

Jinnah, M. A. (1940, March). Presidential Address to Muslim League. *Address by Quiad-i-azam Muhammad Ali Jinnah at Lahore session of Muslim League.* Government of Pakistan, Islamabad. Retrieved April 19, 2022, from http://www.columbia.edu/itc/mealac/pritchett/00islamlinks/txt_jinnah_lahore_1940.html

Jinnah, M. A. (1947, August 11). *First Presidential Address to the Constituent Assembly of Pakistan.* Retrieved April 5, 2022, from http://www.columbia.edu/itc/mealac/pritchett/00islamlinks/txt_jinnah_assembly_1947.html

Kiss, P. A. (2013). *The First Indo-Pakistani War, 1947-48.* Retrieved December 27, 2021, from www.researchgate.net: https://www.researchgate.net/publication/235932742_THE_FIRST_INDO-PAKISTANI_WAR_1947-48

Kohn, H. (n.d.). *Natioanlism.* Retrieved from Britannica: https://www.britannica.com/topic/nationalism

Miller, D. (1995). *On Nationality.* Oxford Press. doi:10.1093/0198293569.001.0001

Ministry of Home Affairs, GoI. (2005). *Annual Report 2004-05.* New Delhi: Government of India. Retrieved January 12, 2022, from https://www.mha.gov.in/sites/default/files/AnnualReport_04_05.pdf

Pandey, P. (2014). Equality: As A Social Principle Described In Vedic. *Maharshi Sandipani Rashtriya Ved Vidya Pratishthan (MSRVVP), 24.* Retrieved March 28, 2022, from https://msrvvp.ac.in/ved-vidya/24/19_Eng._Priyanka_pande_24.pdf

Park, R. E. (1941, January). The Social Function of war Observation and Notes. *American Journal of Sociology, 46*(4), 551-570. Retrieved April 11, 2022, from http://www.jstor.org/stable/2769923

Ray, S. (2017). Indian National Identity: Post Independance journey in the light of millers theory. *Asia Pacific Journal of Research, 1*(L). Retrieved April 13, 2022, from https://www.researchgate.net/publication/316475769_INDIAN_NATIONAL_IDENTITY_POST_INDEPENDENCE_JOURNEY_IN_THE_LIGHT_OF_

MILLER'S_THEORY

Renan, E. (1990). *Nation and Narration.* (H. K. Bhaba, Ed., & M. Thom, Trans.) New York: Routledge. Retrieved January 18, 2022, from https://english.hku.hk/staff/kjohnson/PDF/engl55_kj_renan_nation.pdf

Seton-Watson, H. (1977). *Nations & States - An enquiry into the origins of nations and the politics of nationalism.* Westview Pr. Retrieved February 9, 2022

Shams, S. (2021, October 29). Deutsche Welle. *DW*. Retrieved May 01, 2022, from www.dw.com/en: https://www.dw.com/en/why-cricket-in-pakistan-is-infused-with-religion-and-nationalism/a-59662660

Smith, A. (1983). Theories of Nationalism (2nd edition). *Duckworth*. Retrieved March 9, 2022, from https://openresearch-repository.anu.edu.au/bitstream/1885/115194/2/b12248873.pdf

Smith, A. D. (1971). Theories of nationalism. Retrieved March 9, 2022, from https://openresearch-repository.anu.edu.au/bitstream/1885/115194/2/b12248873.pdf

Sreevatsa, V. (2022, March 08). *Defence Research and Studies*. Retrieved from www.dras.in: https://dras.in/nations-national-identity-and-nationalism/

Stalin, J. V. (1913, March-May). *Marxism and the National Question.* Retrieved February 9, 2022, from www.marxists.org: https://www.marxists.org/reference/archive/stalin/works/1913/03a.htm#s1

Taneja, N., & Bimal, S. (2016). India's Informal Trade with Pakistan. Retrieved May 3, 2022, from https://think-asia.org/handle/11540/6699#:~:text=The%20analysis%2C%20carried%20out%20on,from%20Pakistan%20USD%200.72%20billion.

Tharoor, S. (1997). *From Midnight to Millennium.*

Tharoor, S. (2018). *What is India?* Penguin.

2. From Multilateralism to Minilateralism- A Conceptual Paradigm

M Abdul Fathah[1]

Abstract

Scholars have always struggled with the dilemma of interdependence in a world where nation-states have been the basic unit of political organization for over two centuries. As the primacy of the states continued and complex powers shift recurred, the initial optimism in a world government has come crashing down. Scholars have since then turned into diplomatic interaction between the states to analyze how they relate to each other and form cooperative international organizations, among them the multilaterals and its new avatar, the minilaterals. Considering that it is not the absence of platforms for the states to relate each other, but their astonishing diversity that concerns us, we must look into efficiency of each one of them and why states have prioritized some above the others.

Keywords: Multilateralism, Nation States, Political Organization, Minilateralism, International Cooperation, Diversity of Interests

Multilateralism- A Historical and Qualitative Perspective

The multilateral institutions since the Second World War have been instituted to formalize global norms and sustain a certain sense of predictability to the international system. Structurally, such forums like the UN and WTO have an institutional format with an independent bureaucracy and delegation from a large number of countries. Miles Kahler (1992), one of the earliest scholars to draw distinction between multilaterals and other forms, argues that the vision of multilaterals since 1945 was driven by increasing decolonization of sovereign small states. The formal institutional designs of most post-war multilaterals were said to supplant the disadvantage emerging and small states have faced from the

1 M Abdul Fathah is a Postgraduate in Political Science from Indira Gandhi National Open University and interns with Defence Research and Studies-Praghna Centre for Research

bilateralism of the 1930s and give comparably better opportunities for those who want to accept greater responsibilities and be established powers

In the qualitative sphere, multilateralism generally involves three features: generalized organizing principles, indivisibility and diffuse reciprocity. Generalized organizing principles involve those principles that do not narrow down to the particularistic interests of each country, but specify certain conducts for 'a class of action' that must be adhered by each nation. Indivisibility requires the member countries to accept that there exist some socially constructed public goods. Diffuse responsibility means that member countries do not expect immediate rewards for their efforts and that they would expect only a 'rough equivalence of the benefits in the aggregate and over time.' These qualities, as listed by Ruggie (1992), is more often contrasted with preferential bilateralism where states are allowed to conduct relations on a case-by-case basis tailored to the needs of both countries and where there is always a balancing of responsibility between them.

To see how these qualities are worked out, we must differentiate between the different understanding of this concept as provided by Wedgwood (2002) i.e., multilateralism in the operation and multilateralism in the authorization. The first category includes countries pooling their resource together, as in the case of military act carried out by a joint force. The later one known as 'diplomatic multilateralism' doesn't involve the participation of all countries, but requires a multilateral institution to grant authority to a state or a small group of states to conduct the operation as was the case of American involvement in the Gulf war. This distinction is important because it allows us to see how some celebrated institutions are more often unilateralism or bilateralism under multilateral cover as has been the case of UN Security council. Questions on Nuclear Non-Proliferation during the Cold War were, for instance, mediated as a bilateral issue between USA and USSR within the larger multinational international order. Putting the qualitative characteristics of multilaterals to test in those situations would give us a hint of why majority of the post-war international multilateral orders have been plagued by instances of bilateralism and unilateralism, a difference that is missed once only superficial quantitative characteristics are analyzed. Critiques against multilateralism could be broadly categorized into two dimensions. The first one given by the realists is that the qualitative characteristics of multilateralism do not fit into the hierarchical power configuration of international system where greater powers avoid being scrutinized by smaller powers. The second one given by the neoliberals problematizes the inefficiencies of large groups with diverse members and conventional multilateral strategy by which norms are to be agreed upon by a large pool of countries. Moises Naim (2009) has thus said that since 192 countries signed the United Nations Millennium Declaration in 2000, no multilateral initiatives have been successfully endorsed and practicalized due to these issues.

These critiques would remain at the center of evaluating why certain states opt for more improvised variety of multilaterals in the form of minilaterals.

Minilateralism- An Improvisation

Minilateralism is a relatively later phenomenon that has come as a result of increasing difficulty in maintaining consensus-based traditional multiculturalism that reduces outcomes to the lowest denominator. They are informal, flexible, functional and voluntary frameworks with varied "situational interests, shared values or relevant capabilities" (Patrick, 2016). Though the number of minilateral forums has spontaneously spiked over the last few years, Minilateralism as a concept has been in existence for a long time in a disguised format. Miles Kahler (1992), writing in the wake of cold war, has assessed how large forms of collective action was morphed into smaller and more informal forms of collaboration between some countries within the post-war multilateral institutions. For him and others, those early forums were a mixture of multilateralism, bilateralism and also minilateralism. Similar assessment was also done by Martin (1992), except that she was primarily thinking about groups within the multilateral organization and not organizations like G-7, formed in 1973 and which is often considered as the first instance of pure minilaterals. Thus, even recent scholarship in the field has characterized minilateralism as just another variant of multilateralism, while others like Stewart Patrick (2015) has called it the "New Multilateralism".

In the quantitative sphere, minilaterals are just a subset of multilateralism, except that they logically point to a lesser number of participants than multilateralism. But the basic purpose behind every minilateral forum is to use the least number of actors (known as the magic number) to achieve the greatest impact on problem-solving in the group formation. This magic number could vary considerably and can be lower as three in the case of trilaterals like Indonesia-Malaysia-Philippines Cooperation (IMPC) and can be higher as twenty in the case of economic groups like G-20. This numeric aspect brings us into the basic qualitative feature of minilateral forums i.e., their relative exclusivity. Contrary to the inclusive approach of multilateralism that comes from their focus on indivisibility and generalized organizing principles, minilateral forums follow a critical mass approach, meaning that they bring to the table only those countries that are relevant and makes the biggest impact on the issue in question. Smaller number of stakeholders further means that they are relatively more flexible and that fewer sets of interests are involved in the forums.

Kenneth Oye (1986) consider minilaterals as solving the difficulties of conditional cooperation in multilateral institutions: lower feasibility of sanctions, lower transparency and control over other's action and inability to identify common interests. It must be emphasized here that the greatest impact of minilaterals is thus in the likeness and robustness of their cooperation and not in the expansiveness of the gains incurred from it as an effective multilateral forum would usually trump in that aspect. As noted by John Chamberlin (1982) in his critique of Olson (1968), collective arrangement of more countries could often produce more superior results as in the case of climate laws and the laws of the sea like the UNCLOS. Olson's argument that the size of the group diminishes optimal amount of collective good only holds when goods are characterized by crowding and not in these instances where efficiency of the goods is directly proportional to the number of those following these laws. Kahler (1992) is thus vindicated that even big powers would make side-payments to encourage other nations to accept their agreement.

The Choice of Informality and Institutionalization

Minilateral forums are also informal and functional- meaning that they typically have a targeted approach to address specific challenges and that they lack institutional processes that are built around rules and drawn-out-negotiations. This ambiguity is beneficial in the sense that "broad aims and vague language provide space to maneuver among members that cannot agree on appropriate actions, even if there is consensus on reasonable interests" (Anuar &Hussain, 2021). Minilaterals often involve treaties that are negotiated, but more or less they have "pledge and review" arrangements where nations take certain commitments and they are then submitted for other country's assessment. This characteristic feature of minilateral has allowed it to be a regular format for governance in domains like outer space, maritime security and cyber security that are increasingly contested and congested. Countries who are averse to abide by formal mechanism have made use of such flexible and functional forums to supplant rival parties as is clearly evident in the case of Lancang-Mekong Cooperation formed by China and Mekong-US partnership under American administration. However, low institutionalization has its own problems in the form of loss of focus, shorter life expectancy and lack of organizing frameworks to coordinate inconsistent and unstructured progress of each member. This issue would loom large in the security sector where certainty of commitments would favour formal security alliances in any day.

The relevance of institutionalization to the efficacy and progress of the group is undisputed that many, including Hardin (1982) in his well authored "Collective Actions", see them as resolving the lack of thick network of mutual interactions in large multilateral regimes. Be that as it may, institutionalization is not and need not be the privilege of multilaterals as studies indicate that the institutionalization of organizations like BRICS has enhanced their effectiveness in the fields of trade and anti-terrorism. Some minilaterals like the India-France-Australia dialogue often conduct assessment of their effectiveness, but such developments have not been institutionalized enough to be counted as a broad pattern. Moreover, the reliance on informal links and inter-personal relationship makes them vulnerable to changes in domestic politics, regional environment and ultimately to buy-ins from the government of the day. Most multilaterals usually have an institutional structure and long-time life expectancy as they are driven by the diffuse responsibility and generalized organizing principles. These principals meant that member states do not see multilaterals as mere functional organizations where they can take advantage of the resources of the other nations, but also as organs of global norm creation and community mediation. Quite contrastingly, the same is a problem for minilaterals as they are no longer able to function when geopolitical advantage of the said country and their ability to contribute to substantial policy issue are diminished. Lack of institutional designs to downsize the group or add an alternative member aggravate the problem. Though fresh minilaterals could be an alternative, they run the risk of duplicating policy efforts.

Disaggregated and Multi-level Focus

Another feature of minilaterals is that they breakdown problems into specific dimensions than addressing the expansive and comprehensive box of global issues at once. In this instance, they can be equated with what Patrick (2015) has called "disaggregated multilateralism" that pursue "global governance in pieces" and result in a "regime complex". A regime complex is not just about a single comprehensive treaty, but a cluster of collaborative activities and arrangements. A relative example can be the prescribed sector-specific accords among a subset of WTO members after the failure of Doha talks on trade liberalization. Multi-stakeholder and 'trans-governmental' cooperation of minilaterals are a further distinction from traditional multilateralism. The cooperation between the countries in the forum increasingly takes place outside the confines of external ministries among the transnational network of government officials, cooperate institutions and NGOs. The newly emerged forum of India-US-UAE-Israel is an epitome of prioritizing non-governmental relations in the form of joint production, business to business collaboration and people to people interaction. They involve private sector, local governments and civil society groups from each country working in partnerships. The emergence of such a feature concurs with the new reality of sovereign states trying to tame the globalization as they continue to disaggregate and their subjects continue to engage independently with elements from other states.

Technical agencies and issue-specific specific experts would score here more than the diplomats whose agency is limited to facilitation.

Questions of Justice and Legitimacy

While these benefits are unprecedented and revolutionary, a broader issue of concern is that the structure of minilateral forums lack procedural justice, face trust deficit from countries that are not part of the group and are morally problematic. Prasanth Parameswaran (2018) has pointed out how negative perceptions of the groups being targeted at some or following the path of unilateralism would hinder legitimacy of all the minilaterals in place. This has plagued organizations such as the Indo-Pacific Quad that have raised concerns among countries like China. Avoiding such trust deficits would require, as stated by Joshua Cohen and Charles Sabel, a process by which countries of the minilateral group could explain the efficacy of their acts to the larger multilateral group of nations who can in turn acknowledge their legitimacy, a kind of "diplomatic multilateralism". Another solution is the "inclusive minilateralism" propounded by Robyn Eckersley (2012) on the question of climate negotiations. They are based on the principle of "common but differentiated representation" within the parameters of UNFCC. All of them however point to harnessing the synergy between multilateralism and minilateralism without each one of the two subverting the work of others.

The Synergy Between Multilateralism and Minilateralism

Even though minilaterals do not strictly pursue the goal of international cooperation and global governance, scholars maintain that they should be considered as a bridge building component of larger multilateral world order. Taking due note of deficiencies in both minilateral and multilateral setup, William Tow (2018) had made it clear that minilaterals shouldn't be seen as "completely replacing existing alliances institutions but as complementing them". Minilaterals could be harnessed to focus on niche areas where not all countries have the ability to focus due to capacity constraints, but which could be later taken up multilateral forums for further institutionalization. Technologically and financially advanced countries could jointly explore potentials for research and development of technologies, interact with cooperative sector and big tech to provide innovative solutions for multilateral institutions to address issues like climate change. Paris negotiations of 2015 were given an unprecedented impetus when US-Chinese agreement on reduction of emissions was finalized in November 2014. If not a minilateral, the agreement signaled how similar exclusive agreements would stimulate dynamism to multilateral process by building trust and exploring potential comprise between countries whose actions count. On the other hand, minilaterals between developing, poor and vulnerable economies would provide them with enough strategic hedge against the domination of bigger interests in multilateral forums.

The fears of multilateral forums becoming obsolete are also rather unwarranted as they are always desired by even minilateral states looking for legitimacy of their actions, information advantage and larger burden sharing. Countries such as US and Russia looking for legitimacy in multilateral forums have recognized minilaterals to explore ties with emerging powers, often using them to bring close allies and neutral friends together under their lead in an attempt to create more expansive diplomatic advantage in multilateral forums. Further, it is the rule-based framework and legally binding treaties of multilaterals like UN Convention on the Law of the Sea that facilitates minilateral cooperation. Simultaneously seeking the efficiency of minilaterals and recognition of multilaterals is often expected not just from a liberal institutionalist perspective, but also from the realist understanding of international relations.

The fates of minilaterals like the Quadrilateral Security Dialogue for security cooperation, Lancang-Mekong Cooperation (LMC) for cooperation in connectivity and infrastructure, and Regional Comprehensive Economic Partnerships Agreement (RCEP) in the domain of economic cooperation are telling examples of the pros and cons emanating from the minilateral revolution. A glance into the developments surrounding them would show instances of their flexibility, multistakeholder focus and robust dividends but also instances where they have shown little compactness vis-à-vis domestic backlash, change in governments and power-shifts. Wholly, development of a new foreign policy toolkit in the form of minilaterals would mean that there are much more options that accommodate the imperatives of different countries. While this work has attempted to draw a conceptual paradigm of the evolution from multilateralism into minilateralism, there is much to be analyzed to see how various groupings engage with each other and how did they relate to geopolitical scenario in which they are formed. They will have bearings upon on how we understand the conceptual world of these foreign policy instruments. More research should explore pathways by which countries could engage with minilateral developments in a way that do not cancel the years of work multilateral groups have undertaken. Preliminary analyses of concrete objectives and their geopolitical effects, periodical assessments and an understanding among the countries on the fate of these forums during a potential crisis are some of the points for the member countries to think about.

References

Anuar, A., & Hussain, N. (2021). *Minilateralism for Multilateralim in the Post-Covid Age.* Singapore: S. Rjaratnam School of International Studies.

Eckersley, R. (2012, May). Moving Foreward in the Climate Negotiations: Multilateralism or Minilateralism. *Global Environmental Politics, 12*(2), 35.

Hardin, R. (1982). *Collective Action.* Baltimore: Johns Hopkins University Press.

Kahler, M. (1992). Multilateralism with Small and Large Numbers. *International Organization, 46*(3), 681-708.

Keohane, R. O., & Jr., J. S. (2012). *Power and Interdependence: World Politics in Transition (Fourth Edition.* Boston: Longman .

Malamud, A., & Viola, E. (2021). Multipolarity is in, multilateralism out: rising minilateralism and the downgrading of regionalism. In D. Nolte, & B. (. Weiffen, *Regionalism Under Stress: Europe and Latin America in Comparative Perspective* (pp. 47-65). New York; Oxon: Routledge.

Martin, L. (1992). The rational choice of multilateralism. In J. Ruggie, *Multilateralism matters: The theory and praxis of an institutional form* (pp. 92-121). New York: Columbia University Press.

Naim, M. (2009). *Minilateralism: The magic number to get real international action.* Retrieved from Foreign Policy: http://foreignpolicy.com/2009/06/21/minilateralism/

Nilsson-Wright, J. (2017). *Creative Minilateralism in a Changing Asia.* Chatham House.

Olson, M. (1968). *The Logic of Collective Action.* New York: Schocken.

Oye, K. (1986). Explaining Cooperation Under Anarchy. In K. Oye, *Cooperation Under Anarchy* (p. 19). Princeton: Princeton University Press.

Parameswaran, P. (2018, February 15). *The limits of minilateralism in ASEAN.* Retrieved from The Straits Times: https://www.straitstimes.com/opinion/the-limits-of-minilateralism-in-asean

Patrick, S. (2015). The New "New Multilateralism": Minilateral Cooperation, but at What Cost? *Global Summitry, 1*(2), 115-134.

Patrick, S. (2016). World Order: What, Exactly, are the Rules? *The Washington Quarterly,* 7-27.

Risse-Kappen, T. (1995). Democratic Peace — Warlike Democracies?: A Social Constructivist Interpretation of the Liberal Argument. *European Journal of International Relations.*

Ruggie, J. (1992). Multilateralism: The anatomy of an institution. *International Organization, 46*(3), 561-598.

Singh, B., & Teo, S. (2020). *Minilateralism in the Indo-Pacific.* New York; Oxon: Routledge.

Tago, A. (2017, August 22). *Multilateralism, Bilateralism and Unilateralism in Foreign Policy.* Retrieved from Oxforde.com: https://oxfordre.com/politics/politics/view/10.1093/acrefore/9780190228637.001.0001/acrefore-9780190228637-e-449?rskey=YFNM6h&result=1

Tow, W. T. (2018). Minilateral security's relevance to US strategy in the Indo-Pacific: challenges and prospects. *The Pacific Review,* 232-244.

Wedgwood, R. (2002). Unilateral actions in a multilateral world. In S. P. Forman, *Multilateralism and US foreign policy: Ambivalent engagement* (pp. 167-189). Boulder, CO: Lynne Rienner.

3. An Inquiry into Nations, National Identity and Nationalism

K Vikas Sreevatsa[1]

All contemporary issues are intrinsically linked to and contested by nations. Hence, in the current climate, an inquiry into nations, national identity and nationalism is pertinent. The sequence of the terms, in the order above, is deliberate. The article will trace literature and attempt to first define a nation, in both a rigid and a loose form. After establishing an understanding of the term 'Nation', it will delve into the notion of national identity. Further it will analyze, the phenomenon of 'Nationalism' with respect to the national movement and the role of nationalism in the post-independence consolidation process.

What Is a Nation?

Hugh Seton-Watson (Seton-Watson, 1977) attempts to define a Nation, "Nation is a community of people, whose members are bound by a sense of solidarity". A nation exists when, not all, but a significant number of people in a community consider themselves to form a nation. By virtue of this definition, even social groups based on ethnicity, linguistics, religion come under the ambit of a nation. These social group are also bound by a sense of solidarity and consider themselves as a collective. On the other end of the spectrum, Stalin in his work "Marxism and the National question" (Stalin, 1913) believes,

A nation is a historically constituted, stable community of people, formed on the basis of a common language, territory, economic life, and psychological make-up manifested in a common culture

But as Stalin asserts, all the elements namely history, community, language, territory, economy, psychology, are a prerequisite to a nation. He states, "It is sufficient for a single one of these characteristics to be lacking and the nation ceases to be a nation". This definition of nation by nature is overtly rigid for the

---

1 Vikas Sreevatsa is pursuing his Postgraduate Course in International Relations and currently undergoing the Research Writing Internship with DRaS-Praghna Centre for Research.

contemporary multicultural world. By virtue of this definition, most of modern day nations would cease to qualify as nations. For Benedict Anderson, (Anderson, 1983), a nation "is an imagined political community - and imagined as both inherently limited and sovereign". Imagined because members of even the smallest nation have no ways of interacting with every other member but are still united under the communion of the nation. Limited as even the largest nations are finite in their territory beyond which lie other nations, and do not imagine themselves "co-terminous with mankind".

Understanding the distinction between Hugh Seton-Watson's approach to defining a nation, and Anderson's definition of nation is crucial. Seton-Watson's definition better exemplifies a social group. Any group of people, who share a vision of commonality are a social group. According to Omar Dahbour (Dahbour, 2002), group identity is the social seed that forms the foundation of the idea of a nation. These social groups could be associated based on ethnicity, linguistics, religion, history, culture, etc. A nation adheres to Anderson definition, of an imagined communion which recognises its right to self-determination (sovereignty) in a specific territorially demarcated space. Not all social groups are sovereign or recognise their right to self-determination. Modern day multi-cultural nation-states, may constitute under them, numerous social groups, under the overall communion of a nation. In a nation, none of the social groups are sovereign, but their communion, the nation, is sovereign. Dissatisfaction with the national arrangement might lead social groups to recognise their right to self-determination, and hence form a separate nation by way of succession movements.

Understanding National Identity

Most nations have under their ambit multiple social groups. Narratives, real or imaginary, have to be construed to give these various social groups, direct stakes, in relation to the nation. These narratives could be drawn historically, culturally, linguistically, religiously, ethnographically, etc. aiding the construction of the National Identity. National Identity can be viewed as an abstract ideologue, dynamic in nature that unites different people of different social groups into an imagined communion of a nation. In diverse societies, constructing a national identity connecting all the diverse social groups to the nation, is a challenging endeavor. In these societies, national identity takes the form of moral values and codes that are humanist in nature. Ideas such as pluralism, secularism, democracy, equality, liberty come under the moral doctrines that bind social groups to the nation. To redeem their right to self-determination, the nation forms a state. The project of nation building involves the state constructing narratives that unites the social groups under the communion of the nation.

National identity is dynamic in nature and changes with time. The changes to the national identity might not be uniformly assimilated across social groups which may lead to frictions. When these changes fall outside the purview of comprehension of social groups, the nation as an entity becomes unstable. The role of the state is the keep track of the changing tides of national identity and constantly construct inclusive narratives.

Nationalism

Nationalism has dual existence, as it precedes and proceeds the nation. It manifests during the national struggle, as a means of social mobilization for the national cause, to realize their rights of self-determination, and during the post-independence period to consolidate the nation. Hence, A. D. Smith (Smith A. , 1983) defines nationalism as,

An ideological movement for the attainment and maintenance of self-government and independence on behalf of a group, some of whose members conceive it to constitute an actual or potential 'nation'

The symbols used to invigorate nationalism could be cultural, linguistic, historical, etc. War and sacrifice are also used as emblems of nationalism. These symbols contribute to the molding of the national identity. Pre- independence nationalism concerns itself with first, delimiting the aspects of the aspiring nation with respect to people as well as territory, second, in empowering the citizenry to their right to self-determination.

Nationalism plays a crucial role in the post-independence consolidation process. But the distinction lies in that nationalism after the formation of the nation is state directed. Han Kohn (Kohn, n.d.) Definition of nationalism better describes post-independence nationalism, as an "ideology based on the premise that the individual's loyalty and devotion to the nation-state surpass other individual or group interests". Post-Independence Nationalism is a virtue of loyalty to the nation. Hence nationalism, post-independence, is directed towards eroding traditional group loyalties and prescribing to national loyalties. Smith (Smith A. D., 1971) in his work details the aspiration of post-independence nationalism as integrating the nationals into a homogenous unit.

Conclusion

Nationalism as a force, constructs a national identity to mobilize people, to bring into existence the nation as an autonomous unit. As nations come into existence, national identity and nationalism keep pace with the changing tides of the nation, to consolidate this new formed political entity. Hence, national identity or nationalism take different shapes depending on the end to be achieved, namely either self-determination, or national consolidation. National identity and nationalism are derived from the nation, as well as given to the nation. As nations change linguistically, ethnically, culturally, etc., so does national identity and nationalism as a phenomenon. The state either responds to the national identity emerging from the nation, or constructs a national identity to assimilate the nation with. The balance between enforcing and embracing change in identities is of crucial importance.

References

Anderson, B. (1983). *Imagined Communities : Reflections on the Origin and Spread of Nationalism.* London: Verso. Retrieved January 10, 2022

Dahbour, O. (2002). National Identity : An argument for the Strict Definition. *Public Affairs Quarterly, 16*(1).

Kohn, H. (n.d.). *Natioanlism.* Retrieved from Britannica: https://www.britannica.com/topic/nationalism

Seton-Watson, H. (1977). *Nations & States - An enquiry into the origins of nations and the politics of nationalism.* Westview Pr.

Smith, A. (1983). Theories of Nationalism 2nd edition. *Duckworth.*

Smith, A. D. (1971). Theories of nationalism.

Stalin, J. V. (1913). Marxism and the National Question. *Prosveshcheniye.*

4. CPEC: Exploring Pakistan as a Reliable Partner for China and its Implications on India

Rohini Saini[1]

Abstract

The China-Pakistan Economic Corridor (CPEC) is a multibillion-dollar economic corridor that will connect China's northwestern region of Xinjiang to the Pakistani port city of Gwadar. CPEC highlights China's long-term geopolitical ambitions in South Asia and the Indian Ocean. However, the pace of this initiative has been hindered since its commencement due to economic downturn, political instability, religious extremism, and terrorism that have gripped Pakistan. Nonetheless, the CPEC has significant security and geopolitical ramifications for India. Issues like India's territorial integrity and militarization of the region and China's naval buildup in the Indian Ocean pose serious challenges to geopolitical interests in the region. In the first section, this paper attempts to analyze the much anticipated role of Pakistan as a reliable partner in fulfilment of China's geoeconomic and geopolitical plans behind CPEC. Secondly, this paper will examine and discuss the implications of CPEC on India, especially the security implications. This analytical paper relies on data from secondary sources such as journal articles, research papers and newspaper articles.

Keywords: CPEC, Economic Corridor, Geopolitics, Security, Indian Ocean, LAC

Introduction

China's Belt and Road Initiative (BRI) is a transcontinental development project that aims to strengthen the global economy by boosting regional connectivity and trade. More than 1700 projects totaling $1 trillion are being implemented under the BRI umbrella, including transportations, power grids, energy storage and distribution systems, and so on. BRI is crucial to China because it expands the market for Chinese goods while cutting the cost of export and import. Marshall W. Meyer argued that BRI is vital to China because it is China's global brand (Meyer &

1 Rohini Saini, holds an MA and M.Phil from University of Jammu.

Zhao, 2019). Furthermore, this is a return-oriented Chinese investment. As a result, it must demonstrate some level of success, and any slowdown might be detrimental to Chinese strategic and economic interests.

And what is critical for the success of BRI is the presence of robust institutions backing the initiative in host countries. Some BRI initiatives are located in difficult geographical and institutional settings. The $62 million China Pakistan Economic Corridor (CPEC), which connects China's BRI land and maritime components, is one of these initiatives. Compared to other projects, China has signaled that CPEC is a priority because it provides China with a direct connection to the Strait of Hormuz and the Arabian Sea. Geographically, CPEC moves from Xinjiang province of China and connects Kashgar with Pakistan at Khunjerab pass. From this mountain saddle by moving along the whole Pakistan's territory, China expects to reach the Gwadar port, an entrance to the Indian Ocean, Arabian Sea and Persian Gulf. The CPEC is also a major cornerstone in China–Pakistan strategic partnership. This project holds great promise for both China and Pakistan, since it will help both countries economically, politically, and strategically, particularly China. First, the CPEC is predicted to reduce China's trade transportation costs by 50%. Second, it will provide China with direct access to countries in West Asia, Central Asia, and Africa. Third, it will aid China's counter-offensive against India in the Indian Ocean region.

The CPEC is expected to link China's Kashgar and Pakistan's Gwadar port. A large chunk of the CPEC will run the length of Pakistan's territory. Given the importance of CPEC to China, the question of whether Pakistan can be a trusted partner in China's Grand Initiative arises. Pakistan is a country that lacks a stable political order and is plagued by corruption and the military's monopoly. The majority of the areas through which the CPEC passes, such as Gilgit-Baltistan and Balochistan, are infected with secessionism and terrorism. The fragile and difficult topography, including snow-capped peaks and the ecologically volatile region of Gilgit-Baltistan are stumbling blocks in the completion of CPEC. Pakistan is already a bankrupt state, so no return can be expected and even the principal amount is at risk. All of these factors have already hampered the progress of numerous CPEC projects.

Nevertheless the CPEC has serious strategic and security implications for India (Rahman et al., 2021). If CPEC proves a success, India will have to face strategic, security and economic threats. First, India's claim over PoK and Gilgit Baltistan will be weakened in the international arena. Second, the PLA will continue to intrude eastern Ladakh in order to secure this crucial CPEC project (Lal, 2020). Third, the increasing concentration of PLA forces in Pakistan is posing a security threat to India's western borders. Fourth, CPEC will enable China to expand its naval presence and geostrategic stake in the Indian Ocean. This would put India's regional diplomatic and military capabilities to the test. The focus of this paper will be on two major questions. First and foremost, can Pakistan be regarded as a credible partner in the CPEC's implementation? Second, if CPEC becomes effective, what will be the major implications for India? To begin with, the importance of CPEC to China will be briefly examined.

Literature Review

Sering H. Senge (Senge, 2012) argued that China has started a strategic partnership with Pakistan just to use Pakistan as a security front and a low-cost but high-efficiency deterrent against growing political and economic influence of India in the region. The expansion of the Karakoram corridor will impact the strategic interests of India. This will help Pakistan and China strengthen their military bases near the LOC and allow their armies to infiltrate into Ladakh and the Kashmir Valley swiftly and deeply. By developing this corridor, the Chinese are attempting to encircle India from its northern border. The continuous presence of Chinese workers in Pakistan along India's western border is another challenge. China wants to divert India's attention towards this region and keep herself engaged in yet another strategic front that is the maritime sphere.

Although CPEC is projected to benefit not just China and Pakistan, but also the surrounding areas. And deteriorating law and order circumstances in Balochistan and FATA, as well as the separatist movement in Gilgit Baltistan and Pakhtunkhwa, and Balochistan, religious extremism, and political instability, have continually overshadowed the benefits it is expected to provide. Therefore, its success depends on whether Pakistan will deal with those hurdles (Hussain, 2016).

Jeremy Garlick (Garlick, 2018) argues that Chinese investment in CPEC pipelines is less likely to go ahead due to economic, logistical, geographical and security related problems. And China's motivation for developing infrastructure in Pakistan is to offset India's regional dominance in the Indian Ocean Region. The Chinese interest in Gwadar and other IOR ports derives largely out of a geo-positional balancing against India.

The Politico-economic situation in Pakistan has sabotaged the progress of CPEC. Despite corruption accusations, the military establishment continued to increase its hold on matters pertaining to the Pakistani economy. Moreover, most of the coal based projects stalled because of rising debt and cost of coal, and the transport projects are suffering because of viability issues. The CPEC is affected due to an ongoing insurgency in Balochistan and to a lesser extent in the Gilgit Baltistan region. Impact of the Pakistan financial crisis on CPEC can be guessed from the reduced public sector development project budget for CPEC projects. The allocation was dropped to $130 mn USD for 2020-21 from $1.25 bn USD in 2018-

19 (Joshi, 2021).

Pakistani Army's dominance in polity as well as over economy of Pakistan entails a number of complications for Chinese economic interests that can affect the future of China's CPEC investments and their financial sustainability. However, a number of issues have stymied the CPEC, including escalating prices, which are exacerbated in part by the expenditures of securitizing the CPEC. Meanwhile, Pakistan's economy is not growing sufficiently to cover its huge debt obligations. And if the Pakistani economy continues to underperform, Chinese banks may be forced to cover the expenses of the CPEC (Boon and Ong, 2020).

Anshuman Rahul (Rahul, 2018) argued that China through CPEC wants to encircle India by having access to ports of neighboring countries like Gwadar in Pakistan and Hambantota in Sri Lanka. The recent acquisition of a military base in Djibouti along with the transforming of a number of rocks, reefs and atolls in the South China Sea into military bases do signify the Chinese geo-political ambitions. Although as a response India has announced various connectivity projects in South Asia and beyond, but from a strategic perspective the key project would be the development of Andaman and Nicobar Islands as a maritime hub in Bay of Bengal.

Sayantan Halder (Halder, 2015) has argued that the promises done by China's BRI have largely been rhetorical without a proper road map. In fact, Pakistan's economy has performed abysmally low recently and the failed infrastructural experiment in Sri Lanka is known to all. On the contrary, India has responded well to China's plans by designing its own network of developmental projects in different regions like Asia-Africa Growth Corridor, Project Mausam and Spice route, etc. India has not promised anything big but has mapped a modest economic initiative that seems achievable.

Between 2004 and 2017, there were more than 20 violent strikes on Chinese nationals working in Pakistan. And it seems to have detrimental effects on the prospects of the China–Pakistan economic corridor (CPEC). Nonetheless, China and Pakistan have gradually moved towards deeper cooperation during recent years in spite of continuous risk of attacks. The main explanatory factor apart from security priorities and economic potential is strategic interests. Sino-Pakistani cooperation was founded on a shared goal of countering India and balancing the influence of America in the region (Basit, 2018).

Analysis

In March 2013, Xi Jinping announced his epic vision to make 'China Great Again'. China is leveraging its soft power to strengthen connections with neighbors through infrastructure diplomacy, earning strategic goodwill in the process (Rahul, 2018). CPEC is not just an economic project but also has clear political and security ramifications. Although CPEC has been boasted by both China and Pakistan to boost economic regionalism and connectivity, it is a twin-dimensional endeavor to safeguard its geostrategic sphere, which has both a continental and a maritime component (Saran 2015).

CPEC and China's gains

The motivations for rolling up CPEC are both economic as well as political goals. Creating physical infrastructure will assist cut transportation times and costs, while establishing soft infrastructure will allow for a greater range of items to be exchanged with fewer regulatory impediments. It will also give Beijing a much-needed alternate energy supply route, decreasing its existing reliance on the unpredictable and US-influenced route across the South China Sea.Energy transportation via this route currently takes around 45 days, which may be cut to less than 10 days if done via Gwadar Port. It is expected that transportation costs of all the Chinese trade via sea will also be reduced by 50%. As a result, the Gwadar–Xingjian route can be used as an alternative route for the transportation of energy, which will be time and cost effective (Ahmed et al., 2020).

The corridor would provide China with enormous benefits since it would increase the number of trading routes connecting China to other regions. It will enable China to import energy and find new markets for its products in Central Asia, Africa, and the Middle East. Strategically located near the Strait of Hormuz, Gwadar port represents both a new economic gateway and a military opportunity for Beijing. In future, should China develop a navy robust enough to project credible power into the Indian Ocean, then the port will help Beijing to directly shape events in the Persian Gulf (Ahmad & Hong, 2017). The corridor could help spur economic development in the landlocked western interior of China, as the creation of overland economic connectivity with Central Asia will boost growth there.

Part 1: Pakistan as a reliable partner for

China's Dream of CPEC

The China-Pakistan Economic Corridor (CPEC) is expected to deliver economic prosperity in the whole region. But the realization of the various potential developmental benefits is contingent on the effective completion of the several projects. The development of a corridor in the region must be economically feasible and should offer a satisfactory return on the investment. And its success is also dependent on political stability as well as regional security. CPEC runs along the entire length of the Pakistani territory, which itself faces a myriad of problems

(Sial & Pak Institute for Peace Studies, 2014). This raises the most crucial question: how practical is the realization of such a mega-project in a developing, politically unstable country with an exceptionally inadequate institutional, political, and administrative infrastructure?

Political Instability and Lack of Consensus

Pakistan's domestic politics has never been stable where military and civilian leaders alternate in political authority. Infact, Military controls all the major political and economic decisions. Due to the absence of civilian supervision, there is still secrecy and lack of transparency surrounding the CPEC projects and routes, which is contributing to internal criticism of the project (Vinayak, 2020). Divergence of interests of both the civil and military leadership over distribution of potential benefits of CPEC is further impeding its growth. The political consensus in Pakistan is also weak.There are also divisions between the provinces, particularly Balochistan, Khyber Pakhtunkhwa, and Punjab as well as divisions between the central authority and the provinces over the original route of the CPEC. Due to considerable opposition from regional governments, the Chinese may not be able to finish the Kashgar–Gwadar corridor. Since the inception of the initiative, protests from various parties, especially PTI, have caused delays in its inauguration. Even PTI won the election because of its opposition to the project. It also put light on the fact that people are not in favor of the project.

Mass Protest

The CPEC has remained the center of protest in Pakistan due to China's increasing involvement in Balochistan for squeezing out all the wealth from the region (Bishay, 2021).

The CPEC is viewed by people of Pakistan especially from Gwadar as a foreign occupation of their homeland and an attempt to marginalize the native Baloch people in the guise of economic development (Aamir, 2019). In order to protect Gwadar's port town from insurgents, the government constructed a perimeter security fence with entry checkpoints. The removal of security check posts was one main demand of the massive protests that erupted in Gadar city on 22 November this year. The other reasons being unavailability of basic needs like clean drinking water, electricity, and of course loss of livelihood of fishermen. Such resentments and anti-state feelings may make it impossible for the government to effectively undertake CPEC-projects in the long term. There is a chance of spread of this discontent in other parts of Pakistan considering the way of acquisition of land for infrastructure building. This process can be seen in Punjab province where people have to sell their agricultural land at very low prices. And loss of agricultural land leads again to unemployment as no job has been provided in other sectors.

Poor Governance

The completion of CPEC is hindered by the lack of time and poor management ability on the part of Pakistani authorities. Furthermore, pervasive corruption, a lack of planning and management, such as land acquisition issues and poor development on various projects, have already substantially increased expenses. Pakistani officials have previously stated that several projects planned by China and Pakistan in 2010 may not be completed. While continued energy shortages and inadequate planning will impede CPEC progress and inflate the cost of individual projects.

Security Concerns

As it stands, the intended corridor passes through two of the most volatile parts in this region: Balochistan and the disputed state of Jammu and Kashmir, and the volatility surrounding both ends of this corridor may turn it into a risky venture for Chinese investment. The continuous insurgency in Balochistan province is the most critical impediment to the effective implementation of the CPEC project, as Gwadar port is critical to its success (Aamir, 2019). Moreover, the internal security situation in Pakistan, as well as the link between Pakistan-based terrorist groups and Muslim separatists in western China, is a source of concern for Beijing. Given the extent to which terrorist and militant groups have entrenched themselves in Pakistan, it seems difficult to save the CPEC from them.

Security concerns are among the most pressing concerns about the CPEC (Markey & West, 2016). Despite several anti-terrorism operations, Pakistan's security situation remains perilous (Calabrese, 2016). The main impediment to the completion of CPEC is security. The Baloch insurgents are constantly attacking and kidnapping Chinese con- struction workers and project personnel. In Pakistan's northwest frontier, road networks are planned to run near or through territories where the Pakistani Taliban and other anti-state militant groups could attack construction crews and even disrupt the flow of goods. Although Pakistan claimed that they had eradicated the ETIM from Pakistan, the threat of other militant groups still remains. Baloch insurgent groups, ETIM and TTP have frequently targeted a variety of development projects, blown up infrastructure including gas pipelines, targeted local laborers and civilians, and, most importantly, assaulted Chinese engineers working on the Gwadar project in the framework of CPEC. It appears that providing protection and security to Chinese citizens working on a variety of CPEC-related projects around the country would be a tedious task or a big challenge. Pakistan has deployed nearly 15,000 security personnel to safeguard roughly 7,000 Chinese nationals working on the CPEC (Khan, 2016).

As per analysts, CPEC's security through these forces is feasible in the short term but as CPEC progresses, the presence of Chinese citizens will increase across Pakistan and it will be difficult to provide security to all of them (Shi & Lu, 2016). Recently, the insurgents have escalated the fight beyond Balochistan to avenge their allegation of Chinese exploitation of Balochistan's resources (Joshi, 2021). Four individuals were slain in 2018 when armed gunmen attacked the Chinese consulate in Karachi. In 2020, four people were killed in another attack on the Pakistan Stock Exchange, which is mostly controlled by the Shanghai Stock Exchange. The terror strike on a bus in Dasu on July 14 was notable since it was the first time a large-scale Chinese-financed infrastructure project was attacked (Joshi, 2021).

Economic Concerns

Pakistan's economy is in shambles, with several macroeconomic issues such as expanding current account and budget deficits, falling foreign currency reserves, and unemployment. In 2019, Pakistan's GDP growth rate fell below 1%. Pakistan's economy has been in a catastrophic position, and this will badly affect the implementation of CPEC. Moreover, Pakistan is a semi-industrialized country with few industrial hubs or clusters. The majority of the projected industrial parks are still in the planning stages and would entail significant investment. Similarly, almost all of the missing linkages in the proposed connectivity projects will need massive expenditure. Given Pakistan's perilous economic situation, such a large-scale investment may be unfeasible. Investment in Pakistan has dried up due to a weak law and order situation (Hussain, 2016). While Beijing would pay the majority of the CPEC initiative through commercial loans, soft loans, grants, and private equity investment, Pakistan is also expected to fund transportation projects. However, for nearly one decade, Pakistan's average annual economic growth rate has not been more than 3 percent. Rising militant violence and perpetual political instability have made it difficult for the country to get FDI (Hussain, 2017).

Rising Cost of the Project

The total value of the power and infrastructure deals concluded under CPEC has increased from the $46 billion investment plan originally announced in 2015 to an estimated $62 billion (Hussain, 2017). This rise in costs has resulted from the inclusion of Chinese financing for rail-based mass-transit projects in various other areas. Moreover, the increasing cost of security is becoming a big problem in efficiently pushing forward the project. In 2015, Pakistani authorities decided to create a Special Security Division to defend Chinese interests and nationals in Pakistan (Ritzinger, 2015). And one percent of the cost of CPEC projects was directed towards this cause (Government of Pakistan, 2016).

Undulating and Rugged Topography and Harsh Climates

The northern route of CPEC (Karakoram Highway) passes over challenging mountainous terrain that rises to more than 5000m above sea level and is prone to landslides, extreme weather events, and earthquakes. And parts of the 805 kms track are barely two-way, cut out of the rock face that drops abruptly into valleys below. Due to heavy snow, the Khunjerab Pass stays blocked from November to May; these harsh weather conditions also offer a slew of technical challenges for transportation businesses. Technical alternatives exist, but they are expensive, requiring costly rail and road tunnels as well as pipeline insulation and expensive pumping facilities, raising the project's overall cost (Montesano).

Part 2: Implications for India

As aforementioned in the preceding section, CPEC has several challenges on its path to success. It is hard to believe that the Chinese are seeking to expand infrastructure in Pakistan simply because they have surplus infrastructure capacity and are searching for new markets for their products. While there may be some truth to this, no one takes such huge investment decisions when global demand is slumping (Malik, 2017). The primary rationale for China's participation in Pakistan is obviously geopolitical rather than economic.

The real objective is to balance India by building and maintaining a Chinese presence in India's backyard. The whole approach may be summed up as geo-positional balancing, which seems based on ancient Chinese concepts of geographical space (Callahan, 2008) or strategic encirclement tactics employed in the Chinese game of weiqi (Kissinger, 2011)[1]. Geo-positional balancing is a method of laying down marker stones' in strategic geographical locations for potential future usage and as a hedge against potential disputes (Jeremy, 2018). Raj Verma has also argued that China requires Pakistan just to balance India in South Asia in order to keep the latter distracted, off balance, and entangled in South Asian politics.

Strategic Advantage

The selection of PoK for developing CPEC yields strategic advantages. It will extend China's geographical reach within Pakistan, allowing the PLA to reach extremely close to India's northern and western frontiers Ladakh is crucial for upholding Indian presence on the Siachen Glacier since it allows a physical route to the frozen battlefield and connects it with the rest of the country. And west of the Siachen

1 Weiqi is a popular Chinese strategic board game involving attempts to encircle the opponent, or to resist encirclement by the opponent by putting down black or white stones.

glacier, across the Saltoro Ridge, lies Pakistan controlled Gilgit-Baltistan (Bhatt, 2019). East of it lies China-occupied Aksai Chin. By keeping its presence on the Siachen glacier, India has managed to keep China and Pakistan apart (Storey, 2006). These infrastructure projects under CPEC will consolidate China's control over PoK to tie India down in the region. The Chinese road network via Shaksgam, which connects the Karakoram Highway to the Tibet-Xinjiang Highway, would enclose J&K on three sides (Lee, 2016). While the feeder roads connect significant military complexes in China and Pakistan, Gilgit provides natural cover to military installations such as missile sites and tunnels, increasing their joint capacity and allowing them to undertake collective attack against India (Sering, 2012).

Encirclement of India

China has aggressively followed its policy of "string of pearls" to encircle India (Frankel, 2011). Outposts and airstrips linked by road-rail networks support China's dominant position on the Tibetan plateau to the north. The Xinjiang-Lhasa train link is edging close to Nepal, where China has made considerable political gains. To India's east, China will have access to the Bay of Bengal through transportation and pipeline link to Kyaukpyu port in Myanmar. In the west, CPEC will provide access to the Arabian Sea from Xinjiang via Gilgit-Baltistan to the Gwadar port. Further west, China has established its first overseas military base in Djibouti. To our south, China has constructed Hambantota port in Sri Lanka. So, India's encirclement from the north has been accompanied by a maritime encirclement (Jain, 2017)

Increasing Chinese Influence in India's Ocean

China intended to counter the Indian predominance in the IOR by ensuring its permanent presence in the Indian Ocean. The Indian Ocean Region (IOR) is important in the whole layout of CPEC where Hambantota and Gwadar seaports connect two important dots in the string of pearls strategy (Financial Times, 2017). Additionally, Gwadar has a strategic potential of becoming China's military base. If the Gwadar port is developed into a military base, the Chinese Navy will have a permanent platform in the Indian Ocean (Rehman et al., 2021). If China maintains its naval presence in the Arabian Sea, it may be able to dominate the Strait of Hormuz via the seaport of Gwadar. This would put India's regional diplomatic and military capabilities to the test (Kanwal, 2018).

Many Islands of Lakshadweep are located in the Arabian Sea. And India has been actively conducting many economic zones, exclusive export zones and naval bases in the Arabian Sea (Jain, 2017). Moreover, the assertiveness with which China has acted in the South China Sea can be a reference for India that if China establishes a footing in the Arabian Sea, and hence in the Indian Ocean via Gwadar, it may make national interest claims in India's maritime region as well (Ghiasy & Zhou, 2017). Moreover, it cannot be denied that Beijing's ports in the Indian Ocean will have dual-use facilities, i.e. both economic and military. Such a development will further complicate India's security calculus in the region. To further strengthen its military grip and presence in the Indian Ocean, China is quietly looking to establish a new military base in Jiwani, which is about 80 kms to the west of the Gwadar Port. Such activities undertaken by China in the region and especially near the strategic port are obviously a threat to India's security.

Threat to Energy Security

India is highly dependent on energy imports for its economic growth. India imports with over 60% of its oil supplies passing through the Strait of Hormuz mainly from Saudi Arabia, Iran and Iraq. India has sought to secure shipping lanes for the transportation of oil from the Middle East. Any disruptions in the Indian Ocean can lead to serious consequences for the Indian economy. Located a mere 600 km from the Strait of Hormuz, Gwadar places China in close proximity to the Iran-controlled water channel, which supplies 35% of the world's oil requirements. China's permanent maritime presence at the narrow entrance of the Persian Gulf can be a risk to India's energy security.

Traditional Security Threats

CPEC has the weight to alter the geopolitics of this region. The linking of Karakoram with Gwadar, both having commercial and military significance, can potentially act as strategic choke points with regard to India. The Karakoram ranges are the northernmost and also form the de facto border along which runs the Line of Actual Control (LAC) with China.

As China has already built 36 Kms of road in the Shaksgam Valley and most probably PLA will link the G-219 (Lhasa- Kashgar) highway to Karakoram Pass, through the Shaksgam Pass. This will enable the PLA to put pressure on the (DBO) Daulat Beg Oldi defenses from the North. Once DBO is won by the PLA the route to Siachen via Sasser La Murgo-Sasoma, (Base on Nubra River just south of the Siachen base) can be reached in no time (Lal, 2020).

China has also built 16 airstrips all along Karakoram Highway, mostly for military operations. This would be important for enhancing Pakistan and China's strategic airlift capabilities and ensure smoother logistical support (Prasannan, Ahuja & Sagar, 2021). In the future instance of an India-Pakistan war, China can launch a pincer attack to threaten India and trap its armies in the Ladakh region. China can also keep an eye on the Indian activities in the region by establishing listening posts and advanced surveillance bases in PoK (Gupta, 2017). The route of the CPEC can provide easy transportation of military hardware to Pakistan if the conflict between India and Pakistan rises.

There are apprehensions that terrorist activities will be motivated and will grow more easily because of CPEC because increasing activities along the Indian border will also make PoK more suitable to trespass by terrorists. Recently, the Taliban has also shown interest in joining CPEC. Sawhney* argued that with Kabul likely to join the axis, the military threat will convert into a strategic threat.

Threat to India's Sovereignty

The CPEC route is going through Pakistan-occupied Kashmir (PoK) and Gilgit-Baltistan. Both are Pakistan occupied territories claimed by India and subsequently disregards India's sovereignty (Patil, 2015). If CPEC is a success, it will reinforce the region's status as globally recognised Pakistani territory, undermining India's claim to the 73,000-square-kilometer area. There have also been reports of an increased presence of Chinese troops in the PoK (Chansoria, 2016).

Effect on India's Defence Strategy and Budget

This would also constrain India's plans to reshape its strategic priorities, especially the aim of increasing its maritime capabilities. An increased Chinese military presence on India's northern border could see India shelve or curtail plans for its naval expansion in favor of reinforcing Army and Air Force capabilities. In last year's budget, almost 56% of the total defence outlay was earmarked for the Indian Army. The Air Force and Navy were allocated 23% and 15% respectively.

And in an effort to strengthen its existing continental capabilities, India will soon raise a mountain strike corps primarily in response to rising PLA's presence along India's borders. Questions remain about the three existing strike corps, based in central India and covering Pakistan. Important question is how the mountain corps could be raised within the current allocation of resources for the Indian Army because out of the total allocated budget only 18% constituted capital expenditure while the rest was revenue expenditure. A second problem, the increased Chinese naval presence in the Indian Ocean, means that India is under an obligation to increase the strength of its Eastern Fleet, which may mean shelving the plans for raising the Army's mountain corps (Chandramohan, 2013).

Conclusion

The CPEC is not only the BRI's flagship project but it also plays a key role in Beijing's global ambitions (Adeney and Boni, 2021). Its importance lies in the fact it is a link between the road and Maritime dimensions of China's BRI project. CPEC is expected to reduce the logistical cost and transportation time for Chinese trade by providing a shorter route to the Persian Gulf. It will make China overcome the Malacca Dilemma. Building or operating projects abroad is not merely a security problem; it also involves politics and diplomacy. Apart from geographic location, local support, politics, economic circumstances, security conditions, and people's needs are all variables to consider when choosing a region for project investment. Pakistan's prevailing environment of insecurity which is rife with Islamic militancy and domestic insurgency is posing serious threats to the construction of the corridor (Hassan, 2019). Moreover, Pakistan is a country that lacks a stable political order and is plagued by corruption and the military's monopoly. Pakistan is already a bankrupt state, so no return can be expected and even the principal amount is at risk. There are also mass protests occurring in various parts of Pakistan against CPEC. China needs to approach with caution because things can be turned around unexpectedly. All of these factors have already hampered the progress of numerous CPEC projects. Further, a close assessment of Pakistan's role in implementation of CPEC, Pakistan's position as a reliable partner is highly questionable.

The CPEC can be a serious challenge to India's political, strategic and economic interests, if it becomes a reality. Conventional wisdom has it that India can be worried about CPEC at its two ends: Gwadar, where the Chinese are building a maritime presence, and Pakistan-occupied Kashmir, where Pakistani and Chinese territorial and military frontiers are merging. CPEC looms in on the sovereignty and security of India. Since the inception of the corridor, the concentration of PLAs troops is only on an upwards swing exhibiting rising militarization of the area. The presence of the Chinese military in Pakistan does not fare well with Indian security on its Western borders. The CPEC can be seen as a platform that would allow China to increase its naval presence in the Indian Ocean and to increase their geopolitical stake in the IOR. The Indian Ocean is a significant part of India's national interest and foreign policy. This would become a challenge to India's regional diplomatic and military capabilities.

The best battles are fought at a time and place of your choice (Sinha, 2020). While no one should advocate for war, it seems imperative to be well prepared for it. It would be much better if India could create more political virtual battlefields. India may counter China by dropping its stated stance on the One China Principle and challenging Chinese attempts to dominate maritime choke points. India should continue to strengthen its marine capabilities through cooperative agreements with the United States, France, Japan, and Australia, while also boosting its own military's capacity to protect itself sufficiently. India should also focus on modernizing its technological capabilities like electronic and cyber, Precision Guided Munitions, Space, and other advances.

To protect its most vital assets in the IOR, India should concentrate on a few strategically critical routes and ports along its adjoining seas and islands.

The Andaman and Nicobar Islands should be developed as a modern transit and shipping base. The next step would be to develop Chabahar port in the west with road/rail connections to Central Asia; Trincomalee Port in the east with maritime linkages to Bay of Bengal littoral ports and beyond; and the Mekong-Ganga corridor connecting India's east coast with Indo-China. To secure its northern border, India should work closely with and try to improve relations with its neighbors and also adopt CBMs with Nepal, Bhutan and Myanmar. Along the KKH belt, India should also fortify the whole defense complex of Siachen-DBO-Galwan Valley-Fingers at Pangong Tso since all of these outposts are operational and strategically important. New Delhi should also scale up its defenses along Arunachal Pradesh and Sikkim borders with China and to improve regional connectivity with the North Eastern states.

References

Aamir, A. (February 15, 2019). The Balochistan Insurgency and the Threat to Chinese Interests in Pakistan. f. Retrieved October 26, 2021, from https://jamestown.org/program/the-balochistan-insurgency-and-the-threat-to-chinese-interests-in-pakistan/

Ahmad, R., & Mi, H. (2017). China-Pakistan Economic Corridor and its Social Implication on Pakistan: How will CPEC boost Pakistan's Infrastructures and overcome the Challenges. *Arts and Social Sciences Journal*, 2, 265–273. [Google Scholar]

Ahmad, R., Mi, H., & Fernald, L. W. (2020). Revisiting the potential security threats linked with the China–Pakistan Economic Corridor (CPEC), Journal of the International Council for Small Business, 1(1), 64-80. 10.1080/26437015.2020.1724735

Adeney, K. and Boni, F. (2021). *How China and Pakistan Negotiate.* Carnegie Endowment for International Peace. Retrieved October 22, 2021 from https://carnegieendowment.org/2021/05/24/how-china...

Basit, S. H. (2018). Terrorizing the CPEC: managing transnational militancy in China–Pakistan relations. *The Pacific Review*. 10.1080/09512748.2018.1516694

Bhatt, P. (2019, November). Revisiting China's Kashmir Policy. *Observer Research Foundation, ORF Issue Brief*. 326. Retrieved October 22, 2021, from https://www.orfonline.org/research/revisiting-chinas-kashmir-policy-58128/

Bishay, N. (2021). The Republic World. 'Gwadar ko haq do':Pakistani women, children join protest against China's CPEC project & Imran Khan govt. Retrieved December 2, 2021 from https://www.republicworld.com/world-news/pakistan-news/pakistani-women-children-join-protest-against-chinas-cpec-project-and-imran-khan-govt.html

Boon, H. T., & Ong, G. K. H. (2020). Military dominance in Pakistan and China–Pakistan relations. *Australian Journal of International Affairs.* 10.1080/10357718.2020.1844142

Calabrese, John. (2016, December 20). The China-Pakistan Economic Corridor (CPEC):

Underway and Under Threat. MEI@75. Policy Analysis. Retrieved August 30, 2021, from https://www.mei.edu/publications/china-pakistan-economic-corridor-cpec-underway-and-under-threat#_ftn6

Callahan, William A. (2008). Chinese visions of world order: post-hegemonic or a new hegemony? *International Studies Review*. 10. 751.

Chandramohan, B. (2013, July 16). India's Defence Budget: Implications and Strategic Orientation [*Strategic Analysis Paper*]. Future Directions International. Retrieved October 22, 2021, from https://www.futuredirections.org.au/wp-content/uploads/2013/07/FDI_Strategic_Analysis_Paper_-_16_July_2013.pdf

Chansoria, M. (2016). China's Current Kashmir Policy: Steady Crystallisation. *Journal for the Center of Land Warfare Studies*. 68-80. Retrieved October 12, 2021, from https://claws.in/images/journals_doc/1879857213_2078418284_MonikaChansoria.pdf.

Financial Times. (2017). How China Rules The Wave. Retrieved October 12, 2021 from https://ig.ft.com/sites/china-ports/?mhq5j=e1

Frankel, F. R. (2011). The Breakout of China-India Strategic Rivalry in Asia And The Indian Ocean. *Journal of International Affairs*, 64(2), 1–17. Retrieved October 11, 2021, from http://www.jstor.org/stable/2438553

Garlick, J. (2018). Deconstructing the China Pakistan Economic Corridor: Pipedreams versus Geopolitical Realities. *Journal of Contemporary China*. 10.1080/10670564.2018.1433483

Ghiasy, R. & Zhou, J. (2017). The Silk Road Economic Belt: Considering Security Implications and EU-China Cooperation Prospects. Stockholm International Peace Research Institute. Retrieved October 12, 2021, from https://www.sipri.org/sites/default/files/The-Silk-Road-Economic-Belt.pdf

Government of Pakistan. 2016. *Annual Plan 2016–17*. Islamabad.

Gupta, Brig. A. (2017, Oct 5). Karakoram Highway: A security challenge for India. *Indian Defence Review*. Retrieved October 9, 2021, from http://www.indiandefencereview.com/news/karakoram-highway-a-security-challenge-for-india/

Haldar, S. (2018). Mapping Substance in India's Counter - Strategies to China's Emergent Bett and Road Initiative: Narratives and Counter-narratives. *India Journal of Asian Affairs, 31*(1/2), 75-90. Retrieved September 14, 2021, from https://www.jstor.org/stable/26608824

Hassan, K. (2019). CPEC: A Win-Win for China and Pakistan. Human Affairs, 30. 212–223. 10.1515/humaff-2020-0020

Hussain, Dr. E. (2016). China–Pakistan Economic Corridor: Will It Sustain Itself? *Fudan Journal of the Humanities and Social Sciences, 10*. 10.1007/s40647-016-0143-x

Hussain, Z. (2017, June). The China-Pakistan Economic Corridor and the New Regional Geopolitics. Asie.Visions. 94. Ifri. ISBN: 978-2-36567-738-7. Retrieved October12, 2021, from https://www.ifri.org/sites/default/files/atoms/files/hussain_china_pakistan_economic_corridor_2017.pdf

Jain, S. K. (2017, July). Growing Presence of China in Pak Occupied Kashmir and India's

Concerns. *World Focus, XXXVIII (7)*, 138-141. Retrieved October 11, 2021, from https://www.researchgate.net/profile/Arif-Malik-2/publication/318528293_Rehabilitation_Policy_A_Field_Study_of_PoK_Returnee_Militants/links/5cc46ee1299bf1209784c31c/Rehabilitation-Policy-A-Field-Study-of-PoK-Returnee-Militants.pdf#page=138

Joshi, P., & Vivekananda International Foundation. (2021). China Pakistan Economic Corridor: Domestic Trajectory and Contested Geopolitics. *National Security*, *4*(3), 234- 253. ISSN 2581-9658

Kanwal, G. (2018). Pakistan's Gwadar Port: A New Naval base in China's String of Pearls in the Indo-Pacific. CSIS Brief. Retrieved October 12, 2021, from https://www.csis.org/analysis/pakistans-gwadar-port-new-naval-base-chinas-string-pearls-indo-pacific

Khan, R. (2016, August 12). 15,000 troops of the Special Security Division to protect CPEC projects, Chinese Nationals. *Dawn*. Retrieved October 22, 2021, from https://www.dawn.com/news/1277182

Kissinger, H. (2011). In China. United Kingdom: Penguin Books Limited. 23–25. Retrieved October 21, 2021, from https://www.google.co.in/books/edition/On_China/GldTEJnmbeAC?hl=en&gbpv=1

Lal, A. K. (August 9, 2020). The CPEC challenge and the India-China standoff: An opportunity for war or peace? *Times of India*. Retrieved August 25, 2021, from https://timesofindia.indiatimes.com/blogs/rakshakindia/the-cpec-challenge-and-the-india-china-standoff-an-opportunity-for-war-or-peace/

Lee, P. (2016, May 11). The World's Most Dangerous Letters Are Not SCS…They're CPEC. *China Matters*. Retrieved October 9, 2021, from http://chinamatters.blogspot.com/2016/05/the-worlds-most-dangerous-letters-are.html

Malik, H. Y. (2012). Strategic importance of Gwadar Port. *Journal of Political Studies*, 19(2), 57–69. [Google Scholar]

Malik, A. (2017, May 6). OBOR: For India it is a road to subjugation. *The Pioneer*. Retrieved October 10, 2021, from https://bit.ly/2nTS4CU [Google Scholar]

Markey, D. & West, J. (2016, May 12). Behind China's Gambit in Pakistan. Council on Foreign Relations. *Expert Brief*. Retrieved December 1, 2016, from http://www.cfr.org/pakistan/behind-chinas-gambit-pakistan/p37855

Meyer, M. W., & Zhao, M. (2019, April 30). China's Belt and Road Initiative: Why the Price Is Too High [Podcasts, Whartan Business Daily]. Wharton, University of Pennsylvania. Retrieved October 12, 2021, from https://knowledge.wharton.upenn.edu/article/chinas-belt-and-road-initiative-why-the-price-is-too-high/

Montesano, Francesco S. The China-Pakistan Economic Corridor: Security Challenges at a Geopolitical Crossroads. Retrieved September 20, 2021, from https://www.clingendael.org/sites/default/files/pdfs/The_China_Pakistan_economic_Border_def.pdf

Patil, S. (2015, May 14). OBOR and India's Security Concerns. Gateway House. Retrieved

August 23, 2021, from https://www.gatewayhouse.in/security-implications-of-chinas-transnational-corridors/

Prasannan, R., Ahuja, N. B., & Sagar, P. R. (2021, September 12). Potential axis of Taliban, China and Pakistan could be a cause for worry for India. *THE WEEK*. Retrieved October 19, 2021, from https://www.theweek.in/theweek/cover/2021/09/02/alarming-axis.html

Rahman, Z. U., Khan, A., Lifang, W., & Hussain, I. (2021, January 26). The Geopolitics of the CPEC and Indian Ocean: Security Implication for India. *Australian Journal of Maritime & Ocean Affairs*, 13(3), 122-145. 10.1080/18366503.2021.1875807.

Rahul, A. (2018). The Game for Regional Hegemony: China's OBOR and India's Strategic Response. *Austral: Brazilian Journal of Strategy & International Relations*, *7*(13), 159- 196.

Ritzinger, L. (2015). The China-Pakistan Economic Corridor: Regional Dynamics and China's Geopolitical Ambitions. The National Bureau of Asian Research. Seattle, WA. Retrieved October 26, 2021, from https://www.nbr.org/publication/the-china-pakistan-economic-corridor/

Saran, Amb. S. (2015). What Does China's Global Economic Strategy Mean for Asia, India and The World? Institute of Chinese Studies. Delhi. No. 35. Retrieved from on November 19, 2021, from https://www.icsin.org/uploads/2015/10/09/677d627ad1f9ba3cd77c0bbdd5389f98.pdf

Sering, Senge H. (2012). Expansion of the Karakoram Corridor: Implications and Prospects. *IDSA Occasional Paper No. 27*. 9. Retrieved September 13, 2021, from https://idsa.in/system/files/OP_Karakoramcorridor.pdf

Shi, Z., & Lu, Y. (2016, December 21). The benefits and risks of the China–Pakistan Economic Corridor. Carnegie-Tsinghua Center for Global Policy. Retrieved October 22, 2021, from http://carnegietsinghua.org/2016/12/21/benefits-and-risks-of-china-pakistan-economic-corridor-pub-66507

Sial, S., & Pak Institute for Peace Studies. (2014, July-December). The China-Pakistan Economic Corridor: an assessment of potential threats and constraints. *Conflict and Peace Studies*, *6*(2). Retrieved October 26, 2021, from http://pakistanhouse.net/wp-content/uploads/2016/11/cpec.pdf

Sinha, S. (2020, July 4). Karakoram and other factors in India-China Standoff. *The Sunday Guardian*.

Storey, I. (April 12, 2006). China's Malacca Dilemma. *China Brief*. 6 [8]. The Jamestown Foundation. Retrieved October 9, 2021, from https://jamestown.org/program/chinas-malacca-dilemma/

Vinayak, A. (2020, May 23). *The China-Pakistan Economic Corridor of the Belt and Road Initiative Concept, Context and Assessment by Siegfried O. Wolf, Springer* [Book Review]. Vivekananda International Foundation. Retrieved October 30, 2021,

5. Decoding Taliban and India's Changing Stakes in Afghanistan

Dev Bhatiya[1]

Taliban is a Pashtu word for students. Taliban is a predominantly Pashtun, Islamic fundamentalist group that ruled Afghanistan from 1996 until 2001 until the U.S.-led invasion ousted the Taliban regime for providing refuge to al-Qaeda and Osama bin laden. Founded in 1992 in Southern Afghanistan by one-eyed Islamic cleric - Mullah Mohammad Omar, Taliban managed to capture Kandahar and gained control over Kabul, in 1996 after hanging Mr. Najibullah from a lamppost. At the time, no country in the world recognized the Taliban government in Kabul with the exception of Pakistan, Saudi Arabia and the United Arab Emirates, and during 1996 and 2001, Taliban thrived on Afghan soil.

Osama bin laden the founder of al-Qaeda took refuge in Afghanistan to plan and execute the infamous attack on Twin towers and Pentagon. Taliban and al-Qaeda had very close ties when the Taliban was ruling in Afghanistan. Al Qaeda were supported by the Taliban regime and their logistics came from Pakistan. In words of Major General Ak Siwach (Maj Gen Siwach, 2021) said that Taliban and al-Qaeda were very close to each other, they were two sides of the same coin.

What is the Situation in Afghanistan?

Violence in Afghanistan has been on the rise against the backdrop of the rapid withdrawal of US troops. The US has completed its troops withdrawal, almost ahead of the 20th anniversary of the 9/11 attacks. The Taliban remains a potent force in Afghanistan and is considered crucial in the peace process.

Afghanistan's envoy to India Farid mamudzay had listed out their expectations from India. He had said that India could assist Kabul with military hardware, intelligence & logistics support. India could also assist Afghanistan in financial resources in fighting regional & foreign terrorists. The Ambassador (Laskar, 2021) said:

---

1 Dev Bhatia is a student of Bachelor of Defence and Strategic Studies at Rashtriya Raksha University, Ahmedabad.

> "If we get to a stage where war is imposed on the Afghan public, then we look at India for military and security assistance to protect our people and fight terrorist groups. So, we have not yet got to the stage, we're still giving peace a chance".

How India Has Helped Afghanistan

After US invasion of Afghanistan in 2001, New Delhi got a chance to create an influence inside Afghanistan by making soft power investments without intervening in the political matters. India made substantial investments in developing Afghanistan's infrastructure such as schools, hospitals, dams, roads etc. Salma Dam in Herat testifies India's commitment to economic development and likewise, thirty-six projects India has done for Afghanistan. Some of the major projects are (1) parliament building in Kabul; (2) rebuilding of the Habibia high school; (3) Afghan public institutions with technical advisers; (4) tele-education courses; (5) Zaranj-delaram road and other projects, including dozens of schools and basic health clinics.

India also played a primary role in training Afghan military personnel. Reports say nearly 300 cadets are currently training in India (Negi, 2021)[1]. India also playing an important role in medical treatment of injured Afghan military personnel. Over the year India has supplied seven helicopters to Afghanistan. In the year 2015-16 India supplied four Mi-25 attack helicopters and three cheetah light helicopters. In 2019 India replaced the Mi-25 with four Mi-24v (Roche, 2019) attack helicopters. Earlier Afghanistan had sought offensive military hardware including artillery guns, tanks and armored vehicles.

India's external affairs ministry recently made it clear that New Delhi has no role once projects are completed. India withdrew its ambassador and diplomatic staff from Kabul on August 17 in the view of worsening security situation. However, the Taliban has assured the security of foreign missions and their personnel.

Are US, Russia Favouring Pakistan?

The US military and NATO are in the final stages of withdrawal from Afghanistan. Reports say countries like the US & Russia will favor Pakistan due to its geostrategic location (Umair, 2021). Russia has signed an agreement to build 1,100-kilometer-long gas pipeline from Karachi to Lahore. (AFP, 2021).

India is concerned about presence of Pakistan backed Lashker-e-Taiba and Jaish-e-Mohammad terrorists in Afghanistan. Afghanistan's ties with Pakistan have suffered after kidnap of ambassador's daughter in Islamabad last month. However, appointment of Sarajuddin Haqqani as country's interior minister shows Islamabad's influence and political clout inside Afghanistan. Nevertheless, some segments within Afghanistan including Taliban have openly criticized Pakistan's interference.

Assessment of Crisis

India is assessing the security situation in Afghanistan. Taliban's expansionism is growing concern across the region. US troop's withdrawal has resulted in Taliban's aggressive posturing that has the potential to affect India's security concerns.

India believes Taliban's claim of capturing 85% of Afghan territory is highly exaggerated and it actually controls only 40-50 % of territory mostly in rural parts of Afghanistan (CRUX, 2021) are under Taliban's control. Taliban strategically captured key border points like Spin Buldak in a bid to send out a message that Afghanistan is under their control.

India believes that the hurried US pull-out resulted in gaps in Afghan's air force & intelligence surveillance. International military support is key to counter the Taliban's expansionist attempts. The next 2-3 months are crucial in deciding Afghanistan's future.

India has evidence that Pakistan is providing logistical support to the Taliban. Taliban fighters injured in confrontation with Afghan forces have been treated in Pakistan's Quetta (Laura, 2021). There has been bike rally was conducted in support of Taliban on August there is local support for the insurgent group and over time, they may become stronger. There also been an announcement made in Khyber Pakhtunkhwa province to join the war against Afghan government (CRUX, 2021). Thousands of Taliban fighters seeking refuge in Pakistan Afghan president. Pakistan air force has warned Afghan forces on acting against Taliban – Afghan vice president Amrullah Saleh (Laura, 2021).

Soaring Security Concerns Across Neighborhood

Not just India, China is also concerned about the security in Afghanistan. Afghan situation could fan separatist sentiments among Uyghurs in China. Tajikistan and Uzbekistan are concerned about the humanitarian situation in Afghanistan. India knows that the Taliban provides supports to Pakistan based terror outfits lashkar-e-Taiba & Jaish-e-Mohammed. Owing to Afghanistan's strategic importance and geographical proximity to India, New Delhi is closely watching the developments in Kabul. IIowever, with Taliban sitting in Kabul, New Delhi would have limited say and political influence.

Are Indian Officials Really Involved with Taliban?

According to reports; there have been intermittent contacts between Indian officials and Taliban at different levels in the past few years. Engagement from the Indian side is reportedly being driven by national security advisor, Ajit Doval (TNN, 2021)

India's External Affairs Minister (EAM) S Jaishankar also weighed in on the issue at a recent UNSC debate on Afghanistan. According to him, the report suggests that the intra-Afghan talks have not resulted in a reduction of violence and it has only increased especially after May as the country has been witnessing targeted attacks. The External Affairs Minister said:

> Any political settlement 'in Afghanistan must 'preserve constitutional democratic frame work. India has been supportive of all the efforts being made to accelerate the dialogue between the Afghan government and the Taliban, including the intra-Afghan negotiation. If the peace process is to be successful then it's necessary to ensure that the negotiating parties continue to engage in good faith, eschew the path to find a military solution and fully commit towards reaching a political solution, a tangible demonstration of this commitment is required. (MEA, 2021).

Earlier in June 2021, External Affairs Minister S Jaishankar reportedly made at least two transit halts in Doha, Qatar. During the first halt on June 9, Jaishankar met Qatari National Security Advisor, Mohamed Bin Ahmed Al Meshed. During another transit halt on June 15, the EAM met Qatari foreign minister, Mohammed Bin Abdulrahman Al-Thani. The EAM also held talks with US special envoy Zalmay Khalizad and exchanged perspectives on issues in Afghanistan. However, Indian govt has not officially confirmed the development with Taliban in Doha (MEA, 2021).

What Taliban Wants from India?

Taliban reached out to India for the first time since taking control of Afghanistan. After assuming power in Kabul, a Taliban leader made their first official statement on India. The remarks were made during an interview with Pakistan HUM news channel on August 16. The insurgent group said that it would allow India to complete its reconstruction and infrastructure projects in Afghanistan. During the interview, the Taliban spokesperson added that Indian presence in Afghanistan wouldn't be used against Pakistan. (CRUX, 2021). However, India's role in Taliban-led Afghanistan would be limited and New Delhi may not be able to have the same influence as before. At best, it may try to negotiate with the Taliban for security but it won't be pre-mature to expect much strategic gains and influence.

Kashmir Factor

As per a report, the Taliban has clarified its stand on Kashmir and said it regards it as bilateral and internal issue. The source that spoke to the news agency said Taliban is unlikely to focus in Kashmir (News desk, 2021). This came after an increase in security watch in Kashmir following the group taking power in Afghanistan on august.

The situation had triggered a security threat as groups like *lashkar-e-Taiba* and *lashkar-e-jhangvi* are present in Afghanistan. Both the terror outfits are known for their anti-India operations in Kashmir valley. The scenario New Delhi fears most is the Taliban's victory emboldening terrorist organizations in neighboring Pakistan, endangering India-controlled Kashmir. Indian foreign minister has raised this concern repeatedly in talks with neighboring countries such as Qatar since the U.S. began withdrawing troops in April.

Conclusion

Geographically, Afghanistan is always considered as India's gateway to central Asia. It has always been crucial for India's strategic interests in south Asia also. After Afghanistan was left destroyed in 2001, India helped the country to build roads, schools, hospitals, dams and many other crucial projects to help shape the country's future. With around US$3 billion assistance from India, Afghanistan is one of the largest beneficiaries in South Asia. India has assured support to Afghan government to maintain stability in the country, for a stable Afghanistan is not only important for India but for the whole region. With Taliban's return to power after 20 years of war, the nature of India's engagement with Afghanistan has come into sharp focus. Groups such as the Lashkar-e-Taiba and Jaish-e-Mohammad have been keeping centers and training grounds along the southern provinces of Afghanistan that border Pakistan. With Taliban in power, they appear to have more unrestricted opportunities to carry out attacks against India. Taliban's control will also mean a bigger hand for the Pakistani military and intelligence agencies to influence outcomes for the Afghanistan. Threat for more and more radicalization and its resultant impact on India's internal security emerges as a major concern. This was seen in south Asia in the aftermath of the last withdrawal by foreign troops in Afghanistan in 1990s.

There is also a potential fallout on trade and economy. Impact of radicalization and pro-Pakistan disposition by Taliban, in addition to other terrorist groups mentions, will have adverse impact on on-going Indian projects in Afghanistan. It likely that, trade through Afghanistan under a Taliban regime would be routed through Karachi and Gwadar rather than Chabahar. Even as India accelerates backchannel talks with Taliban, India is also unlikely to officially acknowledge the Taliban government in the near future. However, keeping the strategic implications for India's internal security and its economic interests through Chabahar, it needs to evolve and follow a pragmatic solution towards Taliban ruled Afghanistan.

References

AFP. (2021, july 2). All US and NATO troops leave key Afghanistan air base as withdrawal looms. Retrieved august 16, 2021, from SBS News: https://www.sbs.com.au/news/all-us-and-nato-troops-leave-key-afghanistan-air-base-as-withdrawal-looms/671276f7-481e-4cdb-adcd-cd1ea6b4a13

CRUX. (2021, august 18). Taliban wants India to Finish Afghan Projects, says Kashmir A matter between India & Pakistan. https://youtu.be/7EXRN8-NST4

CRUX. (2021, august 18). Taliban wants India to Finish Afghan Projects, says Kashmir A matter between India & Pakistan. Retrieved from h*ttps://youtu.be/7EXRN8-NST4*

CRUX. (2021, july 29). How India VIews Afghanistan Situation Amid Taliban onslaught, US pullout & Pakistan's terror games. URL: https://www.youtube.com/watch?v=hfoUVlGziUs

Laskar, R. H. (2021, july 10*). India can help boost our air power; Afghan envoy. Retrieved august 16,* 2021, from Hindustan Times, URL: https://www.hindustantimes.com/india-news/india-can-help-boost-our-air-power-afghan-envoy-101625860550313.html

Laura. (2021, july 15). Pakist*an Air Force has Warned Afghan forces on acting against Taliban: Afghanis*tan vice-president Amrullah Saleh. Retrieved august 17, 2021, from News WWC, https://newswwc.com/world/pakistan-air-force-has-warned-afghan-forces-on-acting-against-taliban-afghanistan-vice-president-amrullah-saleh/

Laura. (2021, july 15). Pakistan Air Force has Warned Afghan forces on acting against Taliban: Afghanistan vice-president Amrullah Saleh._Retrieved august 17, 202*1, from News WWC: https://newswwc.com/world/pakistan-air-force-has-warned-afghan-forces-on-acting-against-taliba*n-afghanistan-vice-president-amrullah-saleh/

MEA. (2021, june 22). Statement by External Affairs minister at the UN Assistance mission in Afghanistan. Retrieved August 17, 2021, from Ministry of External Affairs:https://www.mea.gov.in/Speeches-Statements.htm?dtl/33937/Statement_by_External_Affairs_Minister_at_the_UNSC_Debate_on_the_UN_Assistance_Mission_*in_Afghanistan_June_22_2021*

MEA. (2021, march 7). Jaishankar, U.S'. special envoy for afghanistan discuss afghan peace talks. Retrieved august 16, 2021, from The Hindu: https://www.thehindu.com/news/international/jaishankar-us-special-envoy-for-afghanistan-discuss-afghan-peace-talks/article34013392.ece

Negi, M. (2021, september 2). India to complete training of Afg*han army soldiers* in its military academies. Retrieved september 7, 2021, from India Today: https://www.indiatoday.in/india/story/india-to-complete-training-of-afghan-army-soldiers-in-its-*military-academies-1848575-2021-09-02*

*News desk. (2021, august 17). 'Bilateral, In*ternal issue': Taliban' clarifies stand on Kashmir. India on guard. Retrieved august 18, 2021, from News18: https://www.news18.com/news/india/taliban-clarifies-stand-on-kashmir-as-bilateral-internal-issue-india-on-guard-4097045.html

Roche, E. (2019, may 17). *India hands over two mi-24 helicopters to Afghanistan. Retrieved august* 15, 2021, from mint: https://www.livemint.com/news/india/india-delivers-a-pair-mi-24-helicopters-to-afghanistan-1558010138018.html

TNN. (2021, June 23). Indian officials engaging with Taliban 'quietly'. The Times of India. Retrieved August 15, 2021, from https://timesofindia.indiatimes.com/india/indian-officials-engaging-with-taliban-quietly/articleshow/83765373.cms

Umair, *J. (2021, may 8). Treacherous Triangle: Afghanistan, India, and Pakistan after* US withdrawal. Retrieved august 16, 2021, from The Diplomat: https://thediplomat.com/2021/05/treacherous-triangle-afghanistan-india-and-pakistan-after-us-withdrawal/

6. Taliban in Afghanistan: India's Security Challenges

Shristi Choudhury[1]

Introduction

Afghanistan, for a long period of time, has been a victim of proxy wars, a land for superpowers to indulge in contests for power, and a ground for religious conflicts and civil wars. Historically, great powers have come and gone trying to establish their dominance but ultimately failing in the end. The recent events showed evidence that twenty years of energy and resources invested in Afghanistan by the USA was an exercise in futility. The swift takeover of the Taliban has various implications on geopolitics, the balance of power, the rise of extremist groups with perceptible impact on global affairs.

Afghanistan, now controlled by a religious fundamentalist Taliban poses several challenges not only for India but also for the countries sharing borders with it. Its northern neighbors, Uzbekistan and Turkmenistan, are working diplomatically while simultaneously signaling they would not tolerate any cross-border migration without permission (Tanya Mehra, 2021). Pakistan, a nation that has hosted a considerable number of Afghans in its land, also says that it will shut its borders in case of a massive refugee influx (PTI, 2021). Afghanistan's degraded economic situation coupled with the fear of reprisals by the Taliban have forced thousands to flee and attempt to seek asylum across its borders. In a scenario such as this, what are India's challenges and what options does it have left? This question remains central to this article.

India has made around $3 billion dollar investment in Afghanistan. From the construction of the parliament house to building the Salma Dam, India has encouraged infrastructural projects in Afghanistan (Betigeri, 2021). It is not just these developmental projects that are under threat but also the strategic and friendly relationship established over time. In order to protect these investments

---

1 Shristi Chaudhury completed her BA Hons in International Relations from Amity University, Noida.

and ties from being jeopardized, India must critically evaluate its challenges and scrutinize its options in Afghanistan. Given the situation, the immediate challenge for India is to ensure the safe evacuation of the Indian diplomats, government personnel, citizens, who have been residing in Afghanistan. To an extent, this task has already been achieved by the Indian government under operation Devi Shakti as more than a hundred Indians were airlifted and brought home safely despite facing deteriorating conditions (PTI, 2021).

However, the refugee dilemma is yet to have a solution. With the US withdrawing its troops and leaving the nation in a vulnerable atmosphere, several powers, especially China and Russia are trying to take advantage of this vacuum. They are attempting to exert their influence over the region to serve their interests politically or economically.

Rise of Terrorism

Seeing that the Taliban have a brutal history of atrocities, observers reckon that the rise of terrorism is a likely-to-happen situation with the newly formed regime (Turak, 2021). The Taliban regime of 1996-2000 shielded and sheltered a well-known terrorist outfit, Al-Qaeda, who designed and executed the 9/11 attacks from Afghan soil. A recent UN report also claimed that Al-Qaeda and other elements have aligned with the Taliban to celebrate the West's withdrawal, marking it as a win for Islam (UNSC, 2021). Presently, Sirajuddin Haqqani, the Haqqani network's head, is now administering police and security along with overseeing law and order. Moreover, past records indicate fatal attacks and heinous crimes that have been engineered by the Haqqani network, either solely or with some support from the Taliban (Dreanzen, 2015). Due to these aspects, speculations are being raised that Afghanistan may once again become a global hub for terrorism with the return of the Taliban. It is feared that the extremist groups having friendly connections with the Taliban will be able to operate in Afghanistan with no hindrance. This indeed will augment the chances of terrorism in the neighboring areas. The rise of Islamic State Khorasan (IS-K) is also anticipated, a group substantially operating in South and Central Asia. This group can potentially manipulate and draw radicalized individuals from India which can indeed pose a grave threat to the country's internal security. Added to this scenario are the prisoners released by the Afghan Taliban from Kabul. It includes members of Al-Qaeda and the ISKP group, some of whom could be traced to the Kerala Islamic State module. (Chauhan, 2021).

The factors indicate the high possibility of rise in terrorism after the Taliban takeover in Kabul.

Involvement of Pakistan

The transfer of power in the hands of the Taliban itself poses a significant threat but with Pakistan involved, the situation for India gets complicated. This is typically due to the long-standing animosity between the two nations. Following the revocation of article 370, the antagonism between India and Pakistan is seen to be on a rise with more radicalization spreading among locals in Kashmir. Various agencies have provided evidence that Pakistan's ISI had links with the Afghan Taliban, Jaish-e-Mohammad (JeM), Laskar-e-Taiba (LeT), and the Haqqani network, along with numerous other extremist groups. It is a matter of concern as these terrorist outfits are expected to function effortlessly from Afghanistan. Recognized among these are a few anti-India groups like JeM and LeT that principally operate with the objective to separate Kashmir from India. Pakistan has always targeted India, particularly Kashmir, to settle previous scores. In the wake of such an event, the ISI's potential to influence the Taliban's activities in a direction that would harm India is exceedingly high. This projection gains credence with one of the former members of the Taliban claiming ISI to be their "powerful watchdog" (Chaudhuri & Shende, 2020). On this account, New Delhi needs to be extra cautious about its internal security.

Also, the Haqqani network operating with skilfully-trained and well-equipped members further constitutes a grave danger (Weinbaum, Weinbaum, & Babbar, 2016). Referring to past events, the Haqqani network had executed strikes against Indian assets. This included the Indian embassy in Kabul with an Afghan envoy having a strong conviction that the ISI was behind the shadows to facilitate their actions. Pakistan ISI presents itself as a big brother with traces of them providing assistance and encouragement to this group for over several years. Hence, the threat constituted by this faction in conjunction with the ISI cannot be ruled out.

Pakistan's primary goal in Afghanistan, although not entirely, is to contain India's influence and involvement in the region. What threatens India's security is Pakistan's willingness to channelize its resources and influence in orchestrating operations to conduct repulsive attacks against India.

China's Growing Footprint

China initiated its diplomatic talks with the Afghan Taliban long before the group gained control over Afghan soil. Succeeding the significant talks between the Taliban and the US, Chinese officials meeting the Taliban representatives were deemed as another striking move. Foreign minister and state councilor of China, Wang Yi, met with Mullah Baradar and his delegation on July 28, 2021 (Ministry of Foreign Affairs, 2021). This indicates that Beijing might continue to maintain its warm engagement with the Taliban. This anticipation can further be solidified because of two more factors. One, China wants to get their hands on the minerals like iron ore and copper that are enormously present in Afghanistan. Two, with an intention of lining up gigantic projects that could benefit Chinese investors. Either way, it will increase China's presence in the area that might be a little uncomfortable for India given Indo-China's hostile background.

China seems to be cautious about the spread of influence of the East Turkestan Islamic Movement (ETIM) in the Xinjiang region. The insurgency could destabilize the province and turn out to be unfavorable for China (Yang, 2021). Therefore, keeping its national interest in mind, China stands to gain stability in the region in exchange for providing assistance to the Taliban.

In addition, China's focus to secure its interest in the Belt and Road Initiative is robust as well. They have potentially aimed to ensure that the CPEC (China Pakistan Economic Corridor) is carried out smoothly. As a result, it appears that in order to forbid any ETIM from operating from Afghan land and boost its economy, China will continue to maintain friendly ties with the Afghan Taliban. Having a long-standing border conflict, India would not want any growing presence of China or for it to have any robust bilateral ties with the Afghan Taliban that could threaten India's security concerns.

There are possibilities of the emergence of a new Pakistan-China-Taliban pact that might go against India's desires and policies. However, political analysts suggest that although China would want to obtain the maximum profits in the region, it will not entirely jump into Afghanistan to fill the gap taking into consideration the past events that resulted from the invasion. Even though there appears to be very little optimism in the present scenario, it is necessary that India must find means to engage constructively with the Taliban and other regional and global players to secure its own interests.

Conclusion

Evidence from the past support that there would be a rise in terrorism with the overthrow of the Ghani regime. There is also a possibility of rise in extremist groups like the ISKP that can radicalise Indians. To aggravate the situation, the Haqqani network and Pakistan's ISI will operate in a way that might go against India's interests. Additionally, the risk arising from Pakistan's influence is more alarming than the activities spread by any other nation. China is focused on obtaining maximum advantage from the region, simultaneously being cautious about the developments. It could get undesirable for India when two of its adversaries, Pakistan and China, are setting forth motions to deepen their footprints. In a nation where India has invested heavily and established friendly ties with non-Talibani leaders it must take well-calculated measures in order to not let everything go down in flames.

References

Betigeri, A. (2021, August 12). Another proxy war in Afghanistan? Retrieved September 10, 2021, from https://www.lowyinstitute.org/the-interpreter/another-proxy-war-afghanistan

Chaudhuri, R., & Shende, S. (2020, July). Dealing With the Taliban: India's Strategy in Afghanistan after U.S. Withdra*wal. Carnegie Endowment. https://carnegieendowment*.org/files/Chaudhuri_Shende_-_Afghanistan.pdf

Chauhan, N. (2021, August 17). Jailed IS members among Indians freed. Hindustan Times. Retrieved October 20, 2021, from https://www.hindustantimes.com/india-news/jailed-is-members-among-indians-freed-101629152279128.html

Dreazen, Y. (2015, August 3). The Taliban's New Number 2 Is a 'Mix of Tony Soprano and Che Guevara.' Foreign Policy. https://foreignpolicy.com/2015/07/31/afghanistan-taliban-war-terrorism-alqaeda-cia-mullahomar-haqqani/

MEA China. (2021, July 28). Wang Yi Meets with Head of the Afghan Taliban Political Commission Mullah Abdul Ghani Baradar. M*inistry of Foreign Affairs of the People's Republic of China. https://www.fmprc.gov.cn/mfa_eng/*zxxx_662805/t1895950.shtml

Mehra, T., & Wentworth, M. (2021, August 27). The Rise of the Taliban in Afghanistan: Regional Responses and *Security Threats. Retrieved September 3, 2021, from https://icct.nl/pu*blication/the-rise-of-the-taliban-in-afghanistan-regional-responses-and-security-threats/

PTI (2021, August 28). Hundred*s From Afghanistan Being Brought To India Despite Challenges: PM Modi. Retrieved September 12, 2021, from https://www.ndtv.com/india-news/prime-minister-narendra-modi-hundreds-f*rom-afghanistan-being-brought-to-india-despite-challenges-2522274

PTI. (2021, September 2). Pakistan shuts key border crossing with Afghanistan. The Hindu. https://www.*thehindu.com/news/international/paki*stan-shuts-key-border-crossing-with-afghanistan/article36248925.ece

Turak, N. (2021, September 9). Terrorism will increase under Afghanistan's newly appointed Taliban government, experts warn. CN*BC. https://www.cnbc.com/2021/09/08/terrorism-to-increase-under-afghanistans-ne*w-taliban-government.html

UNSC- Letter dated 20 May 2021 from the Chair of the Security Council Committee established pursuant to resolutio*n 1988 (2011) addressed to the Presi*dent of the Security Council. (2021, January 1). United Nations Organisation. https://documents-dds-ny.un.org/doc/UNDOC/GEN/N21/107/61/PDF/N2110761.pdf?OpenElement

Weinbaum, M., & Babbar, M. (2016, September). The Tenacious, Toxic Haqqani Network. Middle East Institute Policy Focus Series. https://www.mei.edu/sites/default/files/publications/PF23_WeinbaumBabbar_Haqqani_web_0.pdf

Yang, J. (2021, August 20). *China's Political Calculations and Potential Options in Afghanistan.* The Diplomat. https://thediplomat.com/2021/08/chinas-political-calculations-and-potential-options-in-afghanistan/

7. China, Taiwan and the One China Principle

Anaswara Joy

Abstract

The contemporary world is looking at the China-Taiwan issue as a challenge to democracy and international law. The Communist Party of China seeks to integrate Taiwan within its sovereignty, either peacefully or coercively by the year 2049. There is an overall disagreement to China's approach mainly coming from the USA and its allies. Its strategic ambiguity in dealing with the China and Taiwan has, if anything, complicated peaceful resolution of the issues between these two. Even at the international stage, United Nations on its part tries to maintain formal relations with the PRC while unofficially promoting relations with Taiwan, thereby challenging the Chinese conception of 'One China Principle'. The mainstream arguments appear to have taken a biased approach without examining China's own interpretation of what the One China Principle entails. Using this as a focal point, the paper uses descriptive and analytical methods, relying upon primary and secondary data (such as official government documents), to encapsulate the Chinese arguments in order to evolve possible solutions to the China-Taiwan conflict. This empirical study concludes by looking at peaceful bilateral negotiations and compromise as the only way to reduce tension and conflict, keeping in mind the aspiration of the Taiwanese government and its people.

Key Words: People's Republic of China, Taiwan, One China Principle, Communist Party of China, Kuomintang, America's Strategic Ambiguity, Sovereignty, Integration, USA

Introduction

Taiwan/ Formosa or Republic of China has been an issue of contestation to People's Republic of China ever since the Chinese civil war. The civil war occurred between the Communist Party under the leadership of Mao Zedong and the Nationalist Party, the Kuomintang under Chiang Kai-shek. The Communist Party won the civil war and dismissed the Kuomintang out of Mainland China, establishing the People's Republic of China. The Kuomintang was exiledandthe regime established their own government in Taiwan by 1949. Therefore, the historical context of Taiwan and China's issue regarding the position of Taiwan brings us to the present international context. The concern stems from Taiwan's position as being an integral part of China and this continues to persist till date. The present Chinese government under the leadership of Xi Jinping has sought to integrate Taiwan with mainland China under its One China Principle which states that, there is only the People's Republic of China in opposition to the contestation of two China's i.e., Republic of China represented as Taiwan (White Paper--The One-China Principle and the Taiwan Issue, n.d.). The Communist government of China is persistent to ensure that Taiwan's consolidation takes place by 2049,(Maizland, August 3, 2022) the year which celebrates the centenary of the Communist regime. The Chinese government's claim to Taiwan is legitimate according to the various signatories they have with the international community as well as corresponding to the consensus shared between both the Chinese and Taiwanese government. China holds on to these international agreements to point towards Taiwan being a part of China and China being the sole representer of the Chinese people. There seems to be no official document which gives adherence to Taiwan being an independent nation state. Taiwan nevertheless still claims to be an independent state but only a handful of small countries have recognised its international status. The Cairo Declaration, the Potsdam Proclamation/Declaration, the 26th session Resolution 2758 of the UN, The Joint Communique as well as the controversial 1992 Consensus between China and Taiwan, all point towards Taiwan being an innate part of the People's Republic of China. But the current geopolitical situation has made it difficult for China to ensure peaceful transition and integration. The problem arises with the present Taiwanese democratic government under "Tsai Ing-wen who explicitly endorses the 'Consensus,' (referring to the 1992 Consensus) which implicitly excludes the possibility of Taiwan's independence from China" (Cohen, 2019). Taiwan has established itself to be a democratic country and with the present Taiwanese government, opting to take measures to dismiss China's offer on "one country, two systems" to accommodate Taiwan's current de facto independence and democratic legal system, relations between the two have only strained(Sands, 2019). The pressing issue for China would be to partake in negotiations with the Taiwanese government in order to move ahead with its vision for a peaceful integration in accordance with the One China Principle. Taiwan is a vital asset to China and it would be in China's interest to bring Taiwan into the People's Republic of China at the earliest.

History

The island of Taiwan 1st came to be known in the 1540's as Ilha Formosa, a name given by Portuguese sailors who were passing through the region (Morris). It is accounted that the island's original people were aboriginal Austronesians who were closely related to the Philippines. The Dutch were the 1st to step into Taiwan. They established themselves in Southern Taiwan in 1622 and established the Dutch East India Company. They resorted to employing thousands of Chinese sojourners and traders as well as aborigines. Their presence on Taiwan forced the outgoing Ming dynasty and the new Manchu Qing of China to pay more attention to the island. It was in the context of this new Chinese consciousness of Taiwan that Zheng Chenggong (Koxinga), Chinese military leader of the late Ming period sought to make the island the base of his movement to overthrow the newly founded Qing dynasty in the name of restoring the vanquished Ming. In 1662, the Dutch were defeated by a military force under the command of the Chinese warlord Zheng Chenggong (1624-1662). In place of the Dutch colonial dispensation, Zheng established what he declared to be a vassal state of crumbling Ming China. Thus, the Zheng regime was significant for being the first "state" on Taiwan with a Chinese-style governmental system(Lai, 2008). The dawn of centralized Qing administration of the island came in 1683, and in 1885 it was granted provincial status under the Qing dynasty. Only under the Qing in the mid-seventeenth century was the name "Taiwan" officially adopted to refer to the whole island. In 1895, less than ten years after it was made a province, Taiwan was abruptly ceded by the Qing emperor to Meiji Japan signing the 'Treaty of Shimonoseki'. For the Japanese, this introduced the sudden responsibility to administer a subject population. From1895-1945 Imperial Japan ruled Taiwan. Meanwhile in China, by 1911 the Qing dynasty was overthrown and in 1912 a new Republic of China was established, headed by the Nationalist Party, also known as the KMT (Kuomintang) or GMD (Guomindang). In 1937, Japan under an extremist military faction, invaded China capturing much of the Eastern part ofthe country and imposing a brutal administration that lasted until the end of World War II in 1945. After World War II and the defeat of Japan by the allied forces, Taiwan was turned over to the Republic of China. From 1945 to 1949, the government of the Republic was engaged in a vicious civil war with forces of the Communist Party. The Communists prevailed and established a new People's Republic of China, whereas the Kuomintang established their own government in Taiwan by 1949.

People's Republic of China- One China Principle

After the Communist Party came to power, they established themselves as the only legal government of entire China and its sole legal representative in the international arena. Thus, it brought the old status of the Republic of China to an end. The government of thc PRC claimed to assert and exercise China's sovereignty, including its sovereignty over Taiwan. The One-China Principle is the foundation stone for the Chinese government's policy on Taiwan(White Paper--The One-China Principle and the Taiwan Issue). It shows Taiwan as an inalienable part of the PRC. The State Council Information Office in Beijing issued a white paper on the

"Taiwan Question and the Cause of China's Reunification in the New Era"(Xinhua). This important document was released as a statement to remind the West and the international forum that China will not budge on its position on Taiwan. The White Paper as published by the Communist party, asserts that the One-China principle is universally accepted in the international community and is in accordance with the international norms. The White Paper claims that it is an "indisputable fact supported by history and the law. Taiwan has never been a state; its status as part of China is unalterable,"(China releases white paper on Taiwan question, reunification in new era, 2022). Ever since 1949, the territories on either side of the Straits have been divided and governed separately, with neither side having jurisdiction over the other. The government of the PRC has never ruled Taiwan; and since 1991 Taiwan has witnessed a form of government that has nothing to do with that of the Chinese mainland. This has only instigated the Communist Party of PRC to push forward its claims through diplomatic and military strategies. On January 30, 1995, President Jiang Zemin, made a statement "Adhering to the One-China Principle is the basis and prerequisite for peaceful reunification " (White Paper--The One-China Principle and the Taiwan Issue). Following this statement,the need was to ensure a peaceful reunification of Taiwan into the People's Republic of China. Given the distinct social systems and ideologies between PRC and Taiwan, the White Paper has proposed the 'one country, two system' approach to establish Taiwan's peaceful integration. But there seems to be no adherence to this approach by the Taiwanese government. This alas has caused a stir in the international community especially with the US behind the heels of the China- Taiwan issue. Therefore, the One China Principle is essential to ensure Taiwan's peaceful integration into the PRC and is a major concern for both parties.

Legal Records Pertaining to People's Republic of China's Claim on Taiwan

The Cairo Declaration

The 1943 Cairo Declaration came out of the Cairo Conference which was held among President Franklin Roosevelt of the United States, Prime Minister Winston Churchill of the United Kingdom, and Generalissimo Chiang Kai-shek of the Republic of China with regards to fighting the war to restrain and punish the aggression of Japan. They sought to eject the Japanese forces from all the territories it had conquered, including the Chinese territories, Korea, and the Pacific Islands (U.S. Department of State). The declaration stated "It is their purpose that Japan, shall be stripped of all the islands in the Pacific which she has seized or occupied since the beginning of the first World War in 1914, and that all the territories Japan has stolen from the Chinese, such as Manchuria, Formosa, and the Pescadores, shall be restored to the Republic of China" (Wilson Centre, n.d.).

The Potsdam Declaration

The Potsdam Declaration/Proclamation signed by Republic of China, the United States and Britain in 1945 (later adhered to by the Soviet Union) stipulated that "The terms of the Cairo Declaration shall be carried out." In August of that year, Japan declared surrender and promised in its Instrument of Surrender that it would faithfully fulfil the obligations laid down in the Potsdam Proclamation. On October 25, 1945, the Chinese government recovered Taiwan and the Penghu Archipelago, resuming the exercise of sovereignty over Taiwan.

Japanese Instrument of Surrender

On September 2, 1945 Japan proclaimed the unconditional surrender to the Allied Powers. It stated as follows: "We hereby undertake for the Emperor, the Japanese Government and their successors to carry out the provisions of the Potsdam Declaration in good faith." It called into putting the Potsdam Declaration into effect. (Japanese Instrument of Surrender, n.d.)

According to the Cairo Declaration, Potsdam Proclamation, and Japanese Instrument of Surrender, the United States and the United Kingdom pledged along with Japan that Taiwan and the outlying Penghu Islands would be restored to the ROC. Therefore, following the victory of the Allies in World War II, the ROC government began exercising its sovereignty over Taiwan on October 251945, by accepting a document of surrender from the Japanese army, declaring the restoration of Taiwan as an integral part of the ROC's territory, and restoring ROC citizenship to the people of Taiwan and Penghu.Additionally, establishing a provincial government and arranging elections to choose representatives of the people. Taiwan and Penghu have thus, been a part of the ROC's sovereign territory since 1945.

The 26th session Resolution 2758 of UN

On October 25, 1971, the UN General Assembly passed United Nations Resolution 2758 (XXVI) stating that the People's Republic of China is the only legitimate government of China. The resolution replaced the ROC with the PRC as a permanent member of the Security Council in the United Nations. This Resolution was passed in response to the United Nations General Assembly Resolution 1668 that required any change in China's representation in the UN to be determined by a two-thirds vote referring to Article 18 of the UN Charter. Recalling the principles of the Charter of the United Nations: "Recognizing that the representatives of the Government of the People's Republic of China are the only lawful representatives of China to the United Nations and that the People's Republic of China is one of the five permanent members of the Security Council" (U.N. Resolution 2758, n.d.).

1992 Consensus

The 1992 Consensus was a verbal agreement between China and Taiwan on the One China principle. The meeting was held on November 1992 in Hong Kong.It was between the Association for Relations Across Taiwan Straits, headed by Wang Daohan of China and the Straits Exchange Foundation (SEF) of Taiwan, led by Koo Chen-fu ("1992 Consensus" on "one -China" principle , 2004). The SEF suggested that both sides would adhere to the "one China" principle but reserve rights to interpret the term "one China" differently. This suggestion gave rise to theso-called "One China, different interpretations" concept, one that is later termed"1992 Consensus" by the SEF former official Su Chi (Lin, What is the "92 Consensus?" Analysis of major players' views and implications for future cross-Strait relations , 2008). Beijing refused to sign on to the SEF's proposal of "One China, different interpretations." In response to the SEF's suggestion, the ARATSagreed to the SEF's suggestion of stating the 'One China Principle,' but both sides were to pursue reunification without talking about the political meaning of 'One China' when negotiating over policy affairs of mutual interests(Lin, 2008).

Further talks held in Hong Kong evaluated on to how the SEF was to express the One China principle. It therefore, proposed 8 formulas to display its spirit of mutual understanding. Out of an earnest desire to solve the problem, the ARATS immediately gave a positive response and made matching concessions, agreeing that both sides could express the one China principle through oral declarations and confirming the specific contents of the oral declarations through letters(Shiquan, 2001). A Summary of the Wang-Koo Talks published by the SEF in August 1993 stated that the consensus reached by ARATS and SEF were quite clear: both sides had worked hard to seek common points while reserving differences in explaining the political content of one China ("1992 Consensus" on "One-China" principle, 2004).

Taiwan's approach to Chinese intrusion

The 2020 Taiwanese democratic elections ended in Tsai Ing-wen of the ruling Democratic Progressive Party winning the presidential elections and retaining its legislative majority. She defeated Han Kuo-yu of the Chinese Nationalist Party or Kuomintang (KMT) and commanded 57 percent of the votes. Ever since her election campaign, the party had undergone pressure from the Chinese government.

Taiwan's major political parties are opposed to de-Sinification and are sceptical of PRC's plan regarding Taiwan. On 2nd January 2019, Xi Jinping restated the core PRC position on Taiwan in a speech. He stressed for peaceful unification under "One Country Two Systems" (Templeman, Taiwan's January 2020 ELECTIONS Prospects and implications for China and the United States, 2019). Tsai responded to Xi Jinping within hours, denouncing his definition of the One-China Principle and asserting that the "vast majority of Taiwan-ese . . . resolutely oppose" OC2S (One Country Two Systems). The forcefulness of her rebuttal, and the attention and support across party lines that it received in Taiwan has caught PRC off guard (Templeman, How Taiwan Stands Up To China, 2020).

Tsai administration has been effectively responding to such challenges by setting measures to squash disinformation, ban-government procurement of Chinese communications technology, including services and equipment from Alibaba, Huawei, and Lenovo as well as banning the online-meeting app Zoom. The Ministry of Foreign Affairs Republic of China (Taiwan), state Taiwan as a democratic nation,which enjoys full statehood but is widely commended by the international community and is not part of China nor has ever been under the jurisdiction of the Chinese government. It further states: "Taiwan's sovereignty belongs to the Taiwanese people, and only their democratically elected government can duly represent them. These objective facts will not change even under China's relentless bullying"(From Public Diplomacy Coordination Council, 2019).

The Taiwanese government also rejects the 1992 Consensus as asserted by PRC. They state that Taiwan did not agree with the Mainland's "One China" principle; rather it suggested "One China with respective interpretations" (The 1992 Consensus The Key to Cross-Strait Peace and Prosperity, 2015).

At the Global Taiwan Institute Annual Symposium on October 5th 2022, President Tsai Ing-wen expressed the Taiwanese government's commitment to working with like-minded partners worldwide to defend freedom and democracy. She also stated how China's persistent military activity undermined the Taiwan Strait status quo and encroaches upon Taiwan's sovereignty threatening peace and stability of the Indo-Pacific region (Taiwan Today, 2022).

The re-election of Tsai Ing-wen and the DPP was a significant setback for Xi Jinping's Taiwan policy. Taiwan's democracy stood up well to a relentless CCP pressure campaign intended to sway the outcome of the 2020 elections.

Taiwan's Status as an Independent Nation

Historically, Taiwan was not incorporated as a province of China until 1885. The Chinese claim to Taiwan is compelling given the Cairo as well as the Potsdam Declarations. The declarations as convened by the United States, United Kingdom,

Soviet Union, and China stated that Taiwan would be given to China after the defeat of Japan. But these declarations were not binding to its members (Allied). The argument continues to observe that Taiwan at that time was legally part of Japan and its status would only be changed by Japan as per the San Francisco Peace Treaty of 1951. The question of Taiwan's status and jurisdiction, Article 2 of the San Francisco Peace Treaty stipulates that "Japan renounces all right, title and claim to Formosa and the Pescadores." On April 28, 1952, in accordance with the stipulations of the San Francisco Peace Treaty, the Treaty of Peace between the Republic of China and Japan (also known as the Treaty of Taipei) was signed between the Nationalist government and Japan. The Treaty of Taipei, in dealing with the question of territory, stipulates in its Article 2 a reconfirmation of the statement in the San Francisco Treaty, saying: "It is recognised that under Article 2 of the Treaty of Peace which Japan signed at the city of San Francisco on 8 September 1951 (hereinafter referred to as the San Francisco Treaty), Japan has renounced all right, title, and claim to Taiwan (Formosa) and Penghu (the Pescadores) as well as the Spratley Islands and the Paracel Islands"(Cheng-jung, The San Francisco Peace Treaty and the Lack of Conclusions on Taiwan's International Status, 2001). Hereby there is no mention under whose jurisdiction Taiwan would be under and therefore, its status remains undefined. It is observed that, even if the Allied declarations were binding, they indicated specifically that Chiang Kai-shek's Republic of China, then still in power in China, would be the recipient of the territory. It is not clear that the P.R.C. could succeed to the R.O.C.'s claim in this regard since the R.O.C. government is still in existence. (Carolan, n.d.)

Another argument in favour of Taiwan comes from the Crimea (Yalta) Conference of 1945. The future of Taiwan was partly determined in this Conference. Under the "Territorial Trusteeship" of "World Organizations" of Protocol Proceedings it read: "the acceptance of this recommendation is subject to its being made clear that territorial trusteeship will only apply to (a)existing mandates of the League of Nations; (b) territories detached from the enemy as a result of the present war" (Yalta Conference Agreement, Declaration of a Liberated Europe, 1945). According to this agreement, Formosa, the Pescadores, and other Japanese colonies should be placed under trusteeship after World War Two, because the Cairo Conference decided to strip them off from Japan (Kiantek, 2000).

This indicates to look into the future of Taiwan according to the aims and principles as laid down by the UN Charter. These principles are of self- determination by its inhabitants, by means of a public referendum, which would ask about the direction desired by the inhabitants of the region, before a verdict can be reached. Charter of the United Nations Article 77 (1945) confirmed Crimea Agreement by regulating that "The trusteeship system shall apply to such territories as…b. territories which may be detached from enemy states as a result of the Second World

War." This meant Taiwan should be put under trusteeship after the War (Kiantek, The True Legal Status of Taiwan, 2000). Further, United Nations Charter Article 76 lay down The basic objectives of the trusteeship system, one being- "to promote the political, economic, social, and educational advancement of the inhabitants of the trust territories, and their progressive development towards self-government or independence as may be appropriate to the particular circumstances of each territory and its peoples and the freely expressed wishes of the peoples concerned, and as may be provided by the terms of each trusteeship agreement" (United Nations Charter , n.d.). Thus, both Charters of the UN stipulate Taiwan for having documented evidence for self-determination.

The question for self-determination is crucial, mainly because of the Chinese assertion and claim for Taiwan being part of the People's Republic of China. The United Nation Charter as per Article 4 states that the admission of any state to membership in the United Nations will be affected by a decision of the General Assembly upon the recommendation of the Security Council. There is no consistency and coherence in the definition, criterion and attributes of "state" adopted by the U.N. Security Council for the purpose of membership. It also satisfactorily meets the Montevideo criteria which stipulates that state as an international juristic person should possess (a) a Permanent population (b) a defined territory (c) a stable government and (d) capacity to enter into relations with other states (Montevideo Convention on the Rights and Duties of States, n.d.). Also, it meets the other criteria such as Democracy and State responsibility. Taiwan has control over its internal affairs (Domestic sovereignty) and is able to keep outsiders from operating within its borders or influencing internal decisions (Westphalian sovereignty) (SV, 2008). Undoubtedly Taiwan fulfils those conditions set by the UN Charter.

But, a political entity, which has the four qualifications prescribed in the Montevideo Convention, does not become a state unless and until it declares that it is a state. This requirement is derived from international custom. In state practice, such a declaration may take a formal or an informal form (Chiang, 1999).

Events Advocating Taiwan's Status as Sovereign Nation

The Battle of Kuningtou/ Guningtou(Oct 25, 1949- Oct 27, 1949)

The Battle of Kuningtou was fought over Kinmen in the Taiwan Strait during the Chinese Civil War in 1949 (Battle of Guningtou, n.d.). After the Kuomintang government under Chiang Kai-shek was defeated from mainland China, they relocated to Taiwan along with 1.2 million people. On October 25th 1949, the Communist Party of China tried to take over Kinmen, located in the north-western coast of the island. But they were defeated by the ROC forces and martial law was declared in Taiwan until 1987(History, n.d.).

For Chiang Kai-shek and the Nationalists, the victory secured their stance on Taiwan from Communist invasion and invigorated their cause after a succession of defeats during the previous year (Chen, n.d.).

Therefore, the Battle of Kuningtou indicates the defeat of CCP and ROC's right over Taiwan.

Taiwan's entry into ICAO (1976)

The Convention on International Civil Aviation, drafted in 1944 by 54 nations, led to the creation of the International Civil Aviation Organization (ICAO). It was established to promote cooperation and "create and preserve friendship and understanding among the nations and peoples of the world" (The History of ICAO and the Chicago Convention , n.d.). Taiwan was able to gain a seat at ICAO in the year 1976 (United States Government Publishing Office , 2014). Taiwan's call to be included in ICAO has been increasingly recognized by the international community as an important stakeholder in the international aviation community (Kwo-tsai, 2022). It calls to question USA's interest in the region. Taiwan entry into ICAO would provide US with real time air safety information, especially those emanating from China and the Taiwanese Strait.

1995-1996 Taiwan Strait Crises

The root cause of the crises started on 22 May 1995, when the Clinton Administration announced that President Lee Teng-hui would be granted a visa to visit Cornell University from 8-12 June 1995. While ostensibly a private visit, this was to be the first time a President from the Republic of China on Taiwan had set foot on American soil. China was opposed to Lee's visit and had received repeated assurances from the US State Department that it would not be allowed.These assurances were passed on to President Jiang Zemin by Chinese Foreign Minister, QianQichen. In early May 1995, the US Congress passed majority resolutions urging President Clinton to allow Lee to make a private visit to Cornell because he was 'the President of a model emerging democracy and America's fifth largest trading partner'. For Taiwan, in its contest with China for the hearts and minds of the US Congress, the decision was a great moral victory. Lee Teng-hui said it was Taiwan's 'most remarkable achievement' and it would bring international attention to the separate existence of the Republic of China on Taiwan. Chinese leaders were furious, and perplexed, by America's green light for the Lee visit(Klintworth, n.d.). During the ten months following Lee's visit to Cornell, the United States and China reopened their difficult negotiations over U.S. policy toward Taiwan. The negotiations reached a climax in March 1996, when China displayed a dramatic show of force consisting of military exercises and missile tests targeted near Taiwan, and the United States responded with an equally dramatic deployment of two carrier battle groups. The 1995–96 Taiwan Strait confrontation was the closest the United States and China had come to a crisis since the early 1960s. It saw the era of a new regional order and became a turning point in post–Cold War U.S.-China relations. The confrontation continues to influence Chinese and American security policies and the bilateral relationships between the United States, China, and Taiwan (Ross R. , 2009).

The year 1996 also saw the first official direct presidential elections for the ROC wherein KMT's Lee Teng-hui won the elections and officially took the position of being the president of Republic of Taiwan(History, n.d.).

America's Strategic Ambiguity onthe China-Taiwan issue

The US has been ambiguous in its position on the China-Taiwan issue. They have a functional relation with Taiwan as well as official formal relations with China. Relations between the two states took a major turn after they undertook 3 major joint statements called the Joint Communique.

The Joint Communique

1. Joint Communiqué of the United States of America and the People's Republic of China/ Shanghai Communiqué (February 28, 1972). In 1972, US President Richard Nixonvisited the People's Republic of China and established the framework within which relations between the two countries wouldprogress. The two sides agreed on normalizing relations, respecting sovereignty and non-interference in the internal matters of other States(Joint Communiqué of the United States of America and the People's Republic of China (Shanghai Communiqué Februaray 28, 1972), n.d.). The United States formally acknowledged that "all Chinese on either side of the Taiwan Strait maintain there is but one China". They also recognized Taiwan as part of China and 'reaffirms its interest in a peaceful settlement of the Taiwan question by the Chinese themselves' (Wilson Centre, Digital Archive, International History Declassified , 1972).
2. Joint Communiqué on the Establishment of Diplomatic Relations (January 1, 1979) The United States of America and thePeople's Republic of China in thisCommunique agreed torecognize each other and formally establisheddiplomatic relations from January 1, 1979. The US proceeded by recognizing the Government of the People's Republic ofChina as the sole legal government of China.Within this context, thc people of the UnitedStates alsosought to maintain cultural, commercial, andother unofficial relations with the people ofTaiwan(China on the World Stage: Weighing the U.S. Response, n.d.).

3. Joint U.S.-China Communiqué (August 17, 1982) This Communique reaffirmed the statements made about the Taiwanese issue in the previous communiqué. It re-enforced the statement on respecting each other's sovereignty and territorial integrity and non-interference in each other's internal affairs. Although no definitive conclusions were reached on the issue of arms sale to Taiwan, the United States declared its intent to continue selling arms to Taiwan and to gradually change its level of arms sales consistent with the PRC's militarization of the Taiwan Strait. It declares, "US government states that it does not seek to carry out a long-term policy of arms sales to Taiwan, that its arms sales to Taiwan will not exceed, either in qualitative or in quantitative terms" (The Three U.S.-CHINA Communiques and the Taiwan Relations, n.d.)

The Taiwan Relations Act (April 10, 1979)

The Taiwan Relations Act was passed by the US Congress and signed into law by the President within just three months after the Joint Communique on the Establishment of Diplomatic Relations between US and China. It calls in to"preserve and promote extensive, close, and friendly commercial, cultural, and other relations between the people of the United States and the people on Taiwan, as well as the people on the China mainland and all other people of the Western Pacific area" (H.R.2479 - Taiwan Relations Act, n.d.). The Taiwan Relations Act has played an indispensable role in shaping American policy toward Taiwan and USstrategy in Asia. It has been an effective policy in matters of safeguarding security and commercial interest of the US.Over the past 20 years, the Taiwan Relations Act has allowed the United States to preserve peace, promote freedom, and maintain flexibility in balancing its relations and interests with governments on both sides of the Taiwan Strait(Yates, 1999). Enabling the American Institute in Taiwan (AIT) alongside the Taiwan Relations Act has created a space forpartnership and friendship between the US and Taiwan in terms for it to prosper in the absence of diplomatic relations. (By authorizing the American Institute in Taiwan (AIT) and other provisions, the Taiwan Relations Act created a framework for relations between the U.S. and Taiwan which has enabled their partnership and friendship to thrive in the absence of diplomatic relations.)

The "Six Assurances" to Taiwan (July 1982)

In 1982, during negotiations for the third United States - China Joint Communiqué on Arms Sales to Taiwan, the Taiwanese government presented the United States with six points that were guidelines for USA-Taiwan relations. According to former Ambassador John Holdridge, the United States agreed to these points and later on July 1982 informed the Congress of the agreement. The six points were:

1. The United States would not set a date for termination of arms sales to Taiwan.
2. The United States would not alter the terms of the Taiwan Relations Act.
3. The United States would not consult with China in advance before making decisions about U.S. arms sales to Taiwan.
4. The United States would not mediate between Taiwan and China.
5. The United States would not alter its position about the sovereignty of Taiwan which was, that the question was one to be decided peacefully by the Chinese themselves, and would not pressure Taiwan to enter into negotiations with China.
6. The United States would not formally recognize Chinese sovereignty over Taiwan.(The "Six Assurances" to Taiwan, n.d.).

One China Policy

These Joint Communiques as mentioned above are indicative of USA's One China Policy. The United StatesOne-China policy goes back at least to 1900, but its focus has varied according to circumstances. The United States recognizes the PRC as the sole legal government of China, acknowledging the Chinese position that Taiwan is part of China. Butit does not recognize Chinese sovereignty over Taiwan. Thus, the United States tries to maintain formal relations with the PRC and has unofficial relations with Taiwan. The 'One China' policy has subsequently been reaffirmed by every new incoming U.S. administration. The existence of this understanding has enabled a sense of stability in the Taiwan Strait, allowing both Taiwan and mainland China to pursue their extraordinary political and socioeconomic transitions in relative peace.The United States does not agree with Beijing's claim to sovereignty over Taiwan, nor does it agree with Taipei that the ROC is an independent, sovereign state(Green, 2017).

Five key documents stand out among U.S. policy statements on Taiwan. Among these, since1979, the Taiwan Relations Act (TRA) has had bipartisan support in guiding the policy with a firmfoundation and flexible framework for the maintenance of the relationship with Taiwan.

- Shanghai Communique of 1972
- Normalization Communique of 1979
- Taiwan Relations Act (TRA) of 1979
- Six Assurances to Taipei of 1982
- August 17 Communique (on arms sales) of 1982.

Successive administrations have generally maintained the long-standingU.S. policy with few changes in some important areas. The U.S. 'One China' policy has differed from the PRC's principle on 'One China,' and therehave been questions about whether U.S. policy is one of support, non-support, or opposition tounification or independence. In short, U.S. policy has stressed the process of peaceful resolution,cross-strait dialogue, with the assent of Taiwan's people, and no provocations or unilateralchanges by either side(Kan, 2011).

Analytical Perspective Stipulating PRC's Sovereignty over Taiwan

After analysing the legal documents and history of both the countries, it could be said Taiwan is not legally part of China as the Communist regime claims, as wellas the idea they are projecting out in the international forum. Taiwan is indispensable for China because of its geological location, which, if acquired would increase its influence and power in the South China Sea, thereby threatening power plays especially for the USA.

The first stance, in favour of it not being part of Taiwan comes directly from history. The aboriginals of Taiwan were Austronesians who were closely related to the Philippines. It was only when the Dutch colonised the land in 1622 did,they resort to employing thousands of Chinese sojourners and traders. Taiwan was then passed on to the Ming and Qing dynasties and later the integrated Republic of China. But soon after Taiwan was colonised by the Japanese. After Japan's defeat, legal documents were signed to give back Taiwan to the Republic of China. The Civil war between ROC and the upsurging Communist party saw the defeat of the Kuomintang government. Chiang Kai-shek the leader of ROC relocated to Taiwan along with 1.2 million people. The Battle of Kuningtou/ Guningtou (Oct 25, 1949- Oct 27, 1949) further proves the victory for Chiang Kai-shek against the Communist invasion, thereby reinstating Taiwan as an independent nation. By1996 the first official direct presidential elections were held wherein KMT's Lee Teng-hui won the elections and officially took the position of being the president of Republic of Taiwan.

Taiwan's stance on not being a sovereign part of PRC is not officially backed by the USA. But USA's ambiguity when it comes to China's stance on Taiwan has helped it to take bolder moves to advocate their independent status. Taiwan's entry into ICAO (1976), the 1995-1996 Taiwan Strait Crisis, the Taiwan Relations Act (April 10, 1979) and the "Six Assurances" to Taiwan (July 1982) are all agreements and initiatives made by the US to balance off China's stringent pursual to overtake Taiwan.

The recent visit of Nancy Pelosi, Speaker of U.S. House of Representatives on the 2nd of August 2022 has created new geopolitical implications on US-China-

Taiwan relations. Beijing responded to the visit as a threat and have had military exercises around Taiwan; with Chinese aircraft intruding more frequently across the informal median line which defines the zone of operations on each side. They had sought to use their naval ships to cruise within the Taiwan Straits and around the island itself (Saran, 2022) . The Ministry of Foreign Affairs of the People's Republic of China gave out a statement condemning Pelosi's visit to Taiwan as violating China's sovereignty and territorial integrity, undermining the peace and stability of the Taiwan Strait, and thereby sending the wrong signal to those in Taiwan in favour of independence(Statement by the Ministry of Foreign Affairs of the People's Republic of China, 2022). The United States views Beijing's response as an unwarranted escalation of coercion toward Taiwan and potential evidence of the mainland's intent to pursue a future blockade or amphibious invasion. Longterm, Beijing's military exercises could set a precedent for increased military activity in the Taiwan Strait with greater show of force. Like prior cases of Chinese military escalation during sovereignty disputes, Beijing may be keen to leverage its higher threshold of military conduct to alter the status quo in the Taiwan Strait and seek a new normal of activities that would pull Taiwan closer(Paul Haenle, 2022).

So far, Pelosi's visit has had little impact on the United States' strategic ambiguity towards Taiwan. There have been no formal treaties, communiqués, nor memorandums of understanding that were brokered between the United States and Taiwan to bolster the existing 1979 Taiwan Relations Act. On top of that, Pelosi's visit unnecessarily gave Beijing opportunistic justification to stage unprecedented military drills around Taiwan without having to incur the full force of international opposition(Anthony Toh, 2022).

Documents: Implications of Various Agreements

Year	Agreement/Memorandum	Implication
1945	Potsdam Declaration/ Proclamation and Japanese Instrument of Surrender	Japan surrendered and the ROC government recovered Taiwan as its sovereign part.
1971	the UN General Assembly passed United Nations Resolution 2758 (XXVI)	UNGA recognised PRC as the legitimate government for the whole of China and replaces ROC with PRC as a permanent member of the Security Council.
1972	The 3 Joint Communique between USA and PRC	US President Nixon's visit to PRC led to it formally recognising PRC and acknowledging One China (Taiwan being its part) along with reaffirmingnon-interference.
1979	The Taiwan Relations Act	Partnership with Taiwan in order to safeguard safety and commercial interest for the US.

1982	The "Six Assurances" to Taiwan	Gave Taiwan an assurance in ensuring that the US does not alter the Taiwan Relations Actalong with other consensus related to arms sales and it not formally recognising its stance on One China

Even after signing the Joint Communique with the PRC, USA has shown ambiguity with its policies regarding Taiwan. This type of foreign policy is likely to keep both sides in a stalemate position. Either one pushing each other to take in a full hold on their stance on Taiwan would cause another world war. The question is, can Taiwan really gain independence? If this were to happen and the USA pushed for Taiwan's independence, would it provoke PRC to send in forces across to claim its sovereignty which has been breached upon? PRC is stern about Taiwan being a sovereign part of China and any attempt to take away their territory would mean an attack on PRC. The Communist Party has very well put out statements to ensure its position and that such an attack would not be tolerated. Case being, if war breaks out, consequences for both sides would be greater with the advent of new dynamics like cyber and space coming into play.PRC has no ambit in its mind that Taiwan is its sovereign part. Therefore, it would not plan on an immediate invasion of Taiwan but seek to use, what Thomas Shelling describes as diplomacy of violence. The Chinese strategy is to take a lead on an uprising crisis, while seizing the opportunity to use it to their benefit, in such a way that it is difficult to solve and break through under normal circumstances (Centre For Strategic and International Studies , 2022). Thus, given USA's ambiguity in its relation with Taiwan, it would not push its chances for a war with the PRC. The current global events would not support such a war and it would be unpredictable for both sides to ensure victory with such power politics. Unless, there is no provocation from either end, Taiwan's position in the international forum would remain the same.

Conclusion

PRC sees Taiwan as its indispensable part and with its Anti-secession Law which was passed in 2005, there seems to be no room for negotiations. The law contains 10 articles which asserts Taiwan's unification with mainland China, further stating, any secession movement on their part or there being no other way to ensure peaceful reunification, PRC would be forced to choose violence to achieve its goal(General Policy Archives(1994-2008), 2005). But opting for non-peaceful means would not guarantee China a win, given the staunch 'ambiguous' opposition from the US. It would bring the world's two largest nuclear powers in confrontation leading to another world war with no evident winners. The USA'sposition is to take a neutral stance but with recognition to the potential gains they could acquire from the situation. On one side with the 1st January 1972 agreement, they established official relations with PRC, recognised them as the sole representative of the whole of China and withdrew recognition tothe Republic of China and shifted out their embassy from Taipei. But soon after, in the same year(1979), they signed the Taiwan Relations Act, contradicting their official claims on sole recognition of PRC. They partnered with Taiwan with the intent on keeping PRC's power in check, as well as to ensure their security and commercial interest in the Taiwan Strait. This ambiguous policy of the USA makes it easy for them to exploit the situation but the complexity of the matter has only created a web of unpredictable conditions.

Future conflicts between PRC, USA and Taiwan will continue unless a peaceful solution is brokered upon. This means, either side will have to negotiate and compromise their policies to ensure peace in the Taiwan Strait. One solution would be for Taiwan to accept China's 'One Country, Two System' but with a revised plan which caters to Taiwan's aspirations. The idea 'One Country, Two System' was first proposed in May 1960, by Chairman Mao and was changed a few times to accommodate the current Taiwanese reality. The policy now states to take special conditions with regard to Taiwan and accepts its capitalist system and way of life. It will remain unchanged for a long period of time until full and peaceful integration into the PRC is ensured(A policy of "one country, two systems" on Taiwan). This policy would only work if Taiwan and PRC sat for dialogue and discussed the provisions for such a system. Taiwan would not accept a full integration into Mainland China, so it would only be feasible for the PRC to compromise to remove this clause anddeclare Taiwan as a special administrative zone, which would mean, not a whole but partial integration.

Another solution, would be to formalise the '1992 Consensus'; revamp the consensus and put forth a suitable agreement between the two. The main issue with the consensus was the understanding on what 'One China' meant. On November 3, 1992, Taiwan suggested on an oral release on the interpretation of 'One China' wherein, President Lee Teng-hui on 1st August 1992 stated them adhering to the one China principle but differing on the meaning of 'One China' as insisted upon by PRC(The 1992 Consensus, 2015). This remained just a consensus and no officialdocuments were signed instating the One China different interpretations resolution. Therefore, a discussion and dialogue to formalise a new '1992 Consensus' would prove to be a much better method to end this conflict peacefully.

The China-Taiwan conflict on India is uncertainand the government has been silent on the recent developments concurring from US House Speaker Nancy Pelosi's visit to Taiwan. When questioned on India's stance on the ongoing issue, Ministry of External Affairs (MEA) spokesperson Arindam Bagchi stated "We urge the exercise of restraint, avoidance of unilateral actions to change status quo, de-escalation of tensions and efforts to maintain peace and stability in the region. India's relevant policies are well-known and consistent. They do not require reiteration," India would be in a pickle as it has trade relations with both parties, with bilateral trade with Taiwan amounting up to $5.7 billion in 2020(Harsh V. Pant, 2022).India is also under constant military stress from China regarding the LAC. Thereby, India does not respond to issues pertaining to the China-Taiwan conflict as it is in its best interest. Even if war broke out, India is likely to opt out to join either side and would prefer to remain non-aligned.

Peaceful bilateral negotiations and compromise is the only way to reducetension and conflict in the Taiwan Strait. The PRC seems to be comfortable in stretching out this conflict but this would only cause more harm and a higher risk for war to break out. This would affect the entire world and there might be unforeseeable destruction if not acted upon soon. China needs to take a step down and seek out its integration in a peaceful way keeping in mind the aspiration of the Taiwanese government and its people.

References

"1992 Consensus" on "one -China" principle . (2004, October 13). Retrieved from People's Daily Online : http://en.people.cn/200410/13/eng20041013_160081.html

"1992 Consensus" on "One-China" principle. (2004, October 13). Retrieved from People's Daily Online : http://en.people.cn/200410/13/eng20041013_160081.html

A policy of "one country, two systems" on Taiwan . (n.d.). Retrieved from Ministry of Foreign Affairs of the People's Republic of China : https://www.fmprc.gov.cn/mfa_eng/ziliao_665539/3602_665543/3604_665547/200011/t20001117_697847.html

Anthony Toh, Z. Y. (2022, August 23). Pelosi's Visit to Taiwan and Geopolitics in Asia. Retrieved from S. Rajaratnam School of International Studies: https://www.rsis.edu.sg/wp-content/uploads/2022/08/IP22047-Toh-Yang-Lee-masthead-final.pdf

Battle of Guningtou. (n.d.). Retrieved from Google Arts and Culture : https://artsandculture.google.com/entity/battle-of-guningtou/m04j95t?hl=en

CAROLAN, C. J. (2000, May). The "Republic of Taiwan": A Legal Historical Justification for a Taiwanese Declaration of Independence . Retrieved from https://www.nyulawreview.org/wp-content/uploads/2018/08/NYULawReview-75-2-Carolan.pdf

Carolan, C. J. (n.d.). The "Republic of Taiwan"; A Leagal Historical Justification for a Taiwanese Declaration of Independence. Retrieved from https://www.nyulawreview.org/wp-content/uploads/2018/08/NYULawReview-75-2-Carolan.pdf

Centre For Strategic and International Studies . (2022, October 7). Retrieved from What if.. Alternatives to a Chinese Military Invasion Of Taiwan : https://www.csis.org/analysis/what-if-alternatives-chinese-military-invasion-taiwan

Chen, E. F. (n.d.). Battle of Guningtou: The Republic of China Fights For Survival. Retrieved from Warfare History Network : https://warfarehistorynetwork.com/battle-of-guningtou-the-republic-of-china-fights-for-survival/

Cheng-jung, L. (2001, 09 10). The San Francisco Peace Treaty and the Lack of Conclusions on Taiwan's Internatinal Status . Retrieved from Internet Archives : https://web.archive.org/web/20150313075002/http://www.twhistory.org.tw/20010910.htm

Cheng-jung, L. (2001, 09 10). The San Francisco Peace Treaty and the Lack of Conclusions on Taiwan's International Status. Retrieved from Internet Archive : https://web.archive.org/web/20150313075002/http://www.twhistory.org.tw/20010910.htm

Chiang, Y. F. (1999). State, Sovereignty and Taiwan . Retrieved from Forahan Internatinal Law Journal .

China on the World Stage: Weighing the U.S. Response. (n.d.). Retrieved from Choices Program, Brown University: https://www.choices.edu/wp-content/uploads/2017/08/choices-china-US-china.pdf

China releases white paper on Taiwan question, reunification in new era. (2022, August 10). Retrieved from Embassy of the People's Republic of China in the United Arab Emirates:http://ae.china-embassy.gov.cn/eng/dshd/202208/t20220810_10740528.htm#:~:text=This%20is%20an%20indisputable%20fact,and%20realizing%20China's%20complete%20reunification.

From Public Diplomacy Coordination Council, M. (2019, May 6). MOFA strongly condemns China's unjustifiable interference with Taiwan's participation in the WHA. Retrieved from Leave No One Behind : https://leavenoonebehind.com.tw/en/article.php?content=154664&unit=451

General Policy Archives(1994-2008). (2005, March 29). Retrieved from Minland Affair Council Republic of China (TAIWAN): https://www.mac.gov.tw/en/News_Content.aspx?n=8A319E37A32E01EA&sms=2413CFE1BCE87E0E&s=D1B0D66D5788F2DE#:~:text=The%20%E2%80%9CAnti%2Dsecession%20Law%E2%80%9D%E2%80%94a%20domestic%20law%20unilaterally,by%20China%20to%20achieve%20unification.

Green, M. J. (2017, January 13). What Is the U.S. "One China" Policy, and Why Does it Matter? Retrieved from Centre for Strategic and International Studies : https://www.csis.org/analysis/what-us-one-china-policy-and-why-does-it-matter

H.R.2479 - Taiwan Relations Act. (n.d.). Retrieved from Congress.gov : https://www.congress.gov/bill/96th-congress/house-bill/2479

Harsh V. Pant, S. M. (2022, August 20). India's Taiwan Movement. Retrieved from Observer Researcg Foundation: https://www.orfonline.org/research/indias-taiwan-moment/

History. (n.d.). Retrieved from Government Portal of the Republic of China (Taiwan): https://www.taiwan.gov.tw/content_3.php

History. (n.d.). Retrieved from Government Portal of Republic of China : https://www.taiwan.gov.tw/content_3.php

Japanese Instrument of Surrender. (n.d.). Retrieved from State Historical Society of IOWA: https://iowaculture.gov/sites/default/files/history-education-pss-wwii-japansurrender-transcription.pdf

Joint Communiqué of the United States of America and the People's Republic of China

(Shanghai Communiqué Februaray 28, 1972). (n.d.). Retrieved from Asia for Educators, Weatherhead East Asian Insitute, Columbia University : http://afe.easia.columbia.edu/ps/china/shanghai_communique.pdf

Kan, S. a. (2011, June 3). China/Taiwan: Evolution of the "One China" Policy- Key Statements from Washington, Beijing and Taipei. Retrieved from https://www.everycrsreport.com/files/20110603_RL30341_2a12f8b513bc9e7220a48a56d21b698368647ac3.pdf

Kiantek, D. S. (2000, July 18). The True Legal Status of Taiwan. Retrieved from Taiwan Nation : https://www.taiwannation.com.tw/english2.htm

Kiantek, D. S. (2000, July 18). The True Legal Status of Taiwan . Retrieved from Taiwan Nation : https://www.taiwannation.com.tw/english2.htm

Klintworth, D. G. (n.d.). Crisis Management: China, Taiwan and the United States - the 1995-96 Crisis and its Aftermath. Retrieved from Parliament of Australia : https://www.aph.gov.au/About_Parliament/Parliamentary_Departments/Parliamentary_Library/pubs/rp/RP9697/97rp14

Kwo-tsai, W. (2022, September 14). Why ICAO Needs Taiwan. Retrieved from The Diplomat : https://thediplomat.com/2022/09/why-icao-needs-taiwan/

Lai, J. (2008). Introduction Accounts of Taiwan and Its History Have Been.

Lin, W.-C. (2008, April 11). What is the "92 Consensus?" Analysis of major players' views and. Retrieved from Institute of Mainland Studies, National Sun Yat-sen University: https://www.mac.gov.tw/public/attachment/04116234039.pdf

Lin, W.-C. (2008, April 11). What is the "92 Consensus?" Analysis of major players' views and implications for future cross-Strait relations . Retrieved from Mainland Affairs Council Republic of China (TAIWAN): https://www.mac.gov.tw/public/attachment/04116234039.pdf

Maizland, L. (August 3, 2022). Why China-Taiwan Relations Are So Tense. Council on Foreign Relations .

MOFA strongly condemns China's unjustifiable interference with Taiwan's participation in the WHA. (2019, May 6). Retrieved from The Ministry of Foreign Affairs (MOFA) of the Republic of China (Taiwan): https://en.mofa.gov.tw/News_Content.aspx?n=1329&s=32955

Montevideo Convention on the Rights and Duties of States. (n.d.). Retrieved from University of Oslo: https://www.jus.uio.no/english/services/library/treaties/01/1-02/rights-duties-states.xml

Paul Haenle, N. S. (2022, August 17). How Pelosi's Taiwan Visit Has Set a New Status Quo for U.S-China Tensions. Retrieved from Carnegie Endowment for International Peace: https://carnegieendowment.org/2022/08/17/how-pelosi-s-taiwan-visit-has-set-new-status-quo-for-u.s-china-tensions-pub-87696

Ross, R. (2009). Chinese Security Policy: Structure, Power and Politics. Routledge.

Ross, R. S. (n.d.). The 1995–96 Taiwan Strait Confrontation. Retrieved from Boston College: https://www.bc.edu/content/dam/bc1/schools/mcas/polisci/The%201995-96%20Taiwan%20Strait%20Confrontation%20Coercion,%20Credibility,%20and%20

Use%20of%20Force.pdf

Saran, S. (2022). Taiwan Between Gaints. Retrieved from Centre for Policy Research : https://cprindia.org/wp-content/uploads/2022/08/taiwan.pdf

Shiquan, X. (2001). The 1992 Consensus: A Review and Assessment of Consultations Between the Association for Relations Across the Taiwan Strait and the Straits Exchange Foundation. Retrieved from National Committiee on American Foreign Policy : https://www.ncafp.org/articles/01%20The%201992%20Consensus-%20A%20Review%20and%20Assessment.pdf

Statement by the Ministry of Foreign Affairs of the People's Republic of China. (2022, August 2). Retrieved from http://world.people.com.cn/: http://world.people.com.cn/n1/2022/0802/c1002-32492623.html

SV, M. (2008). Taiwan Imbroglio: A Brazen Violation of U.N. Charter and Its Basic Principles . Retrieved from Taiwan International Studies Quarterly: http://www.tisanet.org/quarterly/4-1-8.pdf

Taiwan Today. (2022 , October 6). Tsai vows to deepen global collaboration in defending freedom, democracy. Retrieved from Taiwan Today : https://taiwantoday.tw/news.php?unit=2&post=226141

Templeman, K. (2019, December). TAIWAN'S JANUARY 2020 ELECTIONS Prospects and implications for China and the United States. Retrieved from Foreign Policy at Brookings: https://www.brookings.edu/wp-content/uploads/2019/12/FP_20191231_taiwan_election_templeman-1.pdf

Templeman, K. (2020). How Taiwan Stand Up To China. Journal of Democracy.

Templeman, K. (2020). How Taiwan Stand Up To China. Journal of Democracy, 91.

Templeman, K. (2020, July 3). How Taiwan Stands Up To China. Retrieved from National Endowment for Democracy and Johns Hopkins University Press: https://muse.jhu.edu/pub/1/article/760089

The "Six Assurances" to Taiwan. (n.d.). Retrieved from Taiwan Document Project: http://www.taiwandocuments.org/assurances.htm

The 1992 Consensus. (2015, July). Retrieved from Mainland Affairs Council, Republic of China (TAIWAN): https://www.mac.gov.tw/public/MMO/MAC/%E6%91%BA%E9%A0%81-%E8%8B%B1(%E5%AE%9A%E7%A8%BF%E7%89%88).pdf

The 1992 Consensus The Key to Cross-Strait Peace and Prosperity . (2015, July). Retrieved from Mainland Affairs Council Republic of China (Taiwan): https://www.mac.gov.tw/public/MMO/MAC/%E6%91%BA%E9%A0%81-%E8%8B%B1(%E5%AE%9A%E7%A8%BF%E7%89%88).pdf

The 1992 Consensus The Key to Cross-Strait Peace and Prosperity. (2015, July). Retrieved from Mainland Affairs Council Republic of China (TAIWAN): https://www.mac.gov.tw/public/MMO/MAC/%E6%91%BA%E9%A0%81-%E8%8B%B1(%E5%AE%9A%E7%A8%BF%E7%89%88).pdf

The History of ICAO and the Chicago Convention . (n.d.). Retrieved from ICAO: https://www.icao.int/about-icao/History/Pages/default.aspx

The Three U.S.-CHINA Communiques and the Taiwan Relations. (n.d.). Retrieved from Portland State University: https://web.pdx.edu/~hpmg/PS468PS568/TheThreeUSChinaCommuniquesAndTheTaiwanRelationsAct.htm

Tsai vows to deepen global collaboration in defending freedom, democracy. (2022, October 6). Retrieved from Taiwan Today : https://www.taiwantoday.tw/news.php?unit=2&post=226141&unitname=Politics-Top-News&postname=Tsai-vows-to-deepen-global-collaboration-in-defending-freedom%2C-democracy

U.N. Resolution 2758. (n.d.). Retrieved from American Insitute in Taiwan : https://web-archive-2017.ait.org.tw/en/un-res-2758-voted-to-admit-communist-china.html

United States Government Publishing Office . (2014, March 14). The Promise Of The Taiwan Relations Act. Retrieved from GovInfo: https://www.govinfo.gov/content/pkg/CHRG-113hhrg87140/html/CHRG-113hhrg87140.htm

U.S. Department of State . (n.d.). Retrieved from https://2001-2009.state.gov/r/pa/ho/time/wwii/107184.htm

United Nations Charter . (n.d.). Retrieved from United Nations : https://www.un.org/en/about-us/un-charter/full-text

White Paper--The One-China Principle and the Taiwan Issue. (n.d.). Retrieved from https://www.mfa.gov.cn/: https://www.mfa.gov.cn/ce/celt/eng/zt/zgtw/t125229.htm

White Paper--The One-China Principle and the Taiwan Issue. (n.d.). Retrieved from https://www.mfa.gov.cn/.

White Paper--The One-China Principle and the Taiwan Issue. (n.d.). Retrieved from Ministry of Foreign Affairs China: https://www.mfa.gov.cn/ce/celt/eng/zt/zgtw/t125229.htm

Wilson Centre. (n.d.). Retrieved from Digital Archive : https://digitalarchive.wilsoncenter.org/document/122101.pdf?v=d41d8cd98f00b204e9800998ecf8427e

Wilson Centre, Digital Archive, International History Declassified . (1972, February 27). Retrieved from JOINT COMMUNIQUE BETWEEN THE UNITED STATES AND CHINA: https://digitalarchive.wilsoncenter.org/document/121325

Xinhua. (n.d.). China releases white paper on Taiwan question, reunification in new era. Retrieved from ENGLISH.GOV.CN: https://english.www.gov.cn/archive/whitepaper/202208/10/content_WS62f34f46c6d02e533532f0ac.html#:~:text=The%20white%20paper%20was%20released,government%20in%20the%20new%20era.

Yalta Conference Agreement, Declaration of a Liberated Europe. (1945, February 11). Retrieved from Digital Archive : https://digitalarchive.wilsoncenter.org/document/116176.pdf?v=aa91dee05174f33bcb0cefd1e4d561eb

Yates, S. (1999, April 16). Executive Summary: The Taiwan Relations Act After 20 Years: Keys to Past and Future Success. Retrieved from The Heritage Foundation : https://www.heritage.org/asia/report/executive-summary-the-taiwan-relations-act-after-20-years-keys-past-and-future-success

8. India-Taiwan Relations: Should India Continue to Stay Neutral?

Sathya Pulukuri[1]

Introduction

India's relations with Taiwan are slowly improving comparatively through commercial ties and cultural exchange. Both India and Taiwan have their economic interests, India's aspiration to be a manufacturing hub in Asia and Taiwan's ambition to transit to an innovation-driven economy. Taiwan shares similar views as India on peace and regional stability, upholding human rights and democratic values, multilateralism and the convergence of India's Act East policy and Taiwan's New Southbound Policy. Both India and Taiwan are looking for more inclusive ties with the US, Japan and other ASEAN (Association of Southeast Asian Nations) countries. India and Taiwan share a mutual security concern over China.

India is currently unable to have formal diplomatic relations with Taiwan due to India's adherence to OCP (One China Policy) and has been maintaining bilateral relations through unofficial mediums. Taiwan's global space was endorsed for its COVID-19 response to the pandemic. There have been many debates to re-evaluate India's commitments and increasingly drive to support and improve ties with Taiwan after the recent Galwan valley clash with China.

Background-India Taiwan Relations

India has had long-standing ties with Taiwan since the pre-independence period. KMT (Kuomintang) KMT Generalissimo Chiang Kai-shek visited British India in 1942 to progress a closer relationship between India and the ROC (Republic of China). However, the dynamics began to change when the CCP (Chinese Communist Party) took over, and Mao Zedong established the PRC (People's Republic of China). Many centralists believed humourising the CCP could help India ensure its national security (Hashmi, 2020). Therefore, India altered its

1 Sathya Pulukuri is a student of BA HONS Political Science at ARSD College, University of Delhi.

recognition from ROC to PRC. Independent India voted to recognise the PRC in 1950, becoming the second non-communist nation to do so. India's decision received massive criticism from KMT leadership and led to a pause in India-Taiwan relations despite relations with China being suspended for 15 years after the 1962 Sino-Indian War. It was only from the 1990s India established unofficial channels with Taiwan.

India's interaction with Taiwan has gained momentum over the past decades. It all began with the Former Prime Minister of India, P. V. Narasimha Rao, launched India's 'Look East Policy' in 1992 after the balance of payments crisis, followed by Taiwan's 'Go South Policy', which primarily focused on ASEAN economies. India signed various agreements with Taiwan in agriculture, civil aviation, economics, technology, railways and education. Taiwan established representative offices- the ITA (India- Taipei Association) and the TECC (Taipei Economic and Cultural Centre) in 1995.

Bilateral investment agreements were signed between Taiwan and India in 2002. Direct flights between Delhi and Taipei began in 2003. In 2004 a trilateral conference was held in the capital city Taipei between India-Japan-Taiwan. To strengthen cultural relations, from 2004, Taiwan started offering scholarships to study Mandarin to Indian students.

Taiwanese legislators and Ma Ying-jeou (former president of the Republic of China) visited India in 2005 and 2006. In 2010 both the countries reduced the visa restrictions and signed degree recognition in higher education MOUs. In 2011 both India and Taiwan signed multiple agreements on trade, customs and cultural cooperation.

Over the last few years, Taiwan External Trade has established four offices (New Delhi, Mumbai, Chennai and Kolkata). For the past two decades India focussed primarily on engaging economic ties with Taiwan. Due to Chinese objections, bilateral relations are only limited to commercial, technological, and limited interaction in cultural exchange, education, and security.

President of Taiwan, Tsai Ing-wen, launched Taiwan's NSP (New Southbound Policy), the third phase of "Go South Policy" in 2016. This policy attempts to increase international outreach and thereby reduce its dependence on China. India occupies a conspicuous place in the NSP and Taiwan's foreign policy in a broader sense. Under Taiwan's fresh eye of interest in the geopolitical scenario. The NSP emphasizes its engagements with India in the Indo Pacific region, India has expanded its Look East Policy to cover a more broad geographical area from East Asia to Island nations in the Pacific. The synergy between the two policies has boosted economic cooperation.

In 2018, India and Taiwan signed a landmark bilateral Investment agreement promoting investment flow and ensuring the protection and safety of Taiwanese investors. India hosted the Taiwan Film Festival in 2018 to promote Taiwanese culture and encourage ties among youth. In October 2018, the National Gandhi Museum of India and Taiwan's Ministry of Culture organised an exhibition on Mahatma Gandhi's teachings in Taipei.

Taiwan Is A Central Hub of Regional Supply Mechanisms.

Recently India and Taiwan are deliberating to sign a $7.5 bn USD deal to set up a Semiconductor Chip Manufacturing Plant. The Indo-Taiwan science and technology cooperation programme initiated many fully funded R&D projects on AI (Artificial Intelligence), 5G, Biotechnology, Cyber Security, Micro/Nano-electronics, Agro and Food Processing Technology, Renewable energy and embedded systems & sensors.

Since the inception of bilateral relations, two-way trade has increased manifolds from $2 bn USD in 2006 to $5.7 bn USD in 2020, recording 185% growth. Between 2018 and 2019, the FDI inflows from Taiwan have increased ten times, the cumulative flows worth $602.35 mn USD from April 2000 to June 2021 (Plus, 2021). India essentially exports organic chemicals and Naphtha, metal and agricultural products and imports solar cells, PVC (polyvinyl chloride), ICT (Information Communication Technology) Products, electrical machinery. Currently, over 200 Taiwanese companies are operating in India.

Recently, in 2020 the Indian government has approved the Taiwanese firms (Foxconn Technology Group, the Wistron Corp and the Pegatron Corp) for the investment of more than $143 bn USD for Smartphone production. (Chaudhary & Horton, 2020)

Ongoing Impediments

The Chinese influence is impeding the relations between India and Taiwan. Strategically, both India and Taiwan have a common security threat: China, which has its roots in China's claims of Indian Territory and its ambition to annex Taiwan respectively.

To begin with, India viewed Taiwan through the Han Chinese lens over time. India has always remained cautious about Taiwan and has had neutral bilateral ties. However, since 2010, India abstained from mentioning the OCP in official documents due to the Tibet issue.

Even in a hypothesised India-Taiwan-China triangle, China has more chances to dominate the bilateral ties between India and Taiwan single-handedly. China is way more advanced in all various fields than India. For instance, science and technology, industrial production and others. However, in the military domain, India does not appear to be a pushover. Hence both countries are always conscious of China's reaction in bilateral relations.

China's relations with India have always been hypocritical. Apart from having border disputes, China continued to develop more profound economic and security ties with Pakistan, like the BRI's (Belt and road initiative) CPEC (China Pakistan Economic Corridor) initiative and its surrounding effects on India. China abstained from supporting India's objection to POK (Pakistan-occupied Kashmir). Both China and India engaged in a series of military face-offs in Ladakh, Doklam and more recently, Galwan Valley. However, after all this, China still expects India to reaffirm India's stance on the Sino-Taiwan Conflict and refrain from having diplomatic relations with Taiwan.

The issue of Taiwan's sovereignty has been more concerned with cross-strait ties. Taiwan has faced the threat of invasion and persuasive unification from the CCP the whole time. But the situation became more intense under Xi Jinping's leadership for so-called 'peaceful reunification'. Recently, Chinese military activities in the Taiwan Strait threatened Taiwan's regional peace and security. Taiwan believes China is impending the bilateral relations so the internal dynamics can advance the ties. (Karackattu, 2019)

Currently, India and Taiwan have no joint mechanism to address the shared security threat as the ties are only limited to economic ties. India has been holding its stance for a long time to settle Chinese aggression.

Nevertheless, India's relations with China are only deteriorating even after having a neutral stance. Therefore, as both countries' relations with China are escalating, India needs to reconsider its commitment to the OCP and extend its relations with Taiwan.

Geopolitics and Convergence Options

Chinese expansionism in recent times led to the emergence of the arc of convergence of strategic interests between the other states. India missed the boat by abstaining from having bilateral relations with Taiwan till the present. Both India and Taiwan are natural allies and share common security concerns and hold similar interests. Through a broader lens, engaging with Taiwan not only accommodates India's growing concerns about China but further promotes trade, technology and R&D cooperation, encouraging cultural and educational activities and Thus, by expanding India's soft power diplomacy. India can expand a strategic partnership, including economic and defence-security cooperation with Taiwan.

The Chinese factor can be a decisive driver for India's cooperation with Taiwan, India can signal coercion to China by providing political and diplomatic support to Taiwan. Taiwan has close geostrategic contiguity and cultural and linguistic links with China. Taiwan invested profoundly in China studies over time. Therefore, Taiwan's expertise can help India understand China's strategic profundity. India's security community can learn mandarin and strengthen their understanding of Chinese culture. Yielding hard and soft cyber capabilities can mitigate cyber-attacks. Strengthening the cooperation does not necessarily mean a military alliance. However, regular information exchange can help both countries to negate possible threats. (Basrur & Shang-Su, 2021)

Taiwan plays a vital role in sustaining stability in the Indian Ocean region due to its significant fishing presence. India can deploy its military attaché to their missions in Taiwan like the U.S. and Japan to have a stronghold in Taiwan Strait and the South China Sea regions. Approximately 55% of India's trade with the Indo-Pacific passes through the South China Sea (Pant, 2021). India can extend its Oil and gas exploration ventures in the region with Taiwan's assistance. India can coordinate with Taiwan to send their regional humanitarian assistance and disaster relief efforts.

Taiwan enjoys a favourable trade balance with China, whereas India's imports from China rose by 67% from the last year (Press Trust of India, 2020) .Therefore, the economic cooperation between both countries can create mutual benefit and reduce dependence on China. Both India and Taiwan have complementary financial arrangements. India's software expertise, along with Taiwan's hardware, can result in mutual interest. India can benefit from high-tech corporations and thereby join the regional supply chain mechanisms.

Technological cooperation like working on space, semiconductors, AI, and 5G can improve its ties with India. Taiwan is willing to converge New Southbound policy with the IPOI (Indo-Pacific Ocean initiatives) to develop some action plans on Maritime Security, Ecology, Capacity building and Resource sharing, technological Cooperation, transportation and others. Taiwan is also willing to be included in SCRI (Supply Chain Resilience Initiative) launched by India, Japan and Australia.

Taiwan is the hub of manufacturing automobiles, hardware, electronics, information and communication technology and others to support India's initiatives (Skill India, Digital India, Smart Cities, and Make in India campaigns). Taiwan's food processing and agro-based technology can help India to modernise its agricultural sector. Hence, India can make use of this technology to produce value-added products.

India can be a new potential base for Taiwan to relocate their manufacturing bases from China. Taiwan is a world-driving semiconductor supplier and technologically advanced. Taiwan ranks number one in integrated circuit foundries and patent activities and number ten in economic innovation globally. Taiwan can support India's digital revolution. Partnering with Taiwanese pharmaceutical companies can significantly lower the high drug prices. Taiwan can provide logistical support for major infrastructure projects in India.

Spiritual intimacy can bring rationality in bilateral relations. India being the birthplace of Buddhism, can promote its soft power diplomacy through Religious tourism. India can use Taiwan as a launchpad into the Indo-Pacific under Act-East policy.

Way Forward

Today's world is reshaping with the evolution of multilateralism and multilateral dialogue, anticipating a normative world order that incorporates and benefits nations. Conscious of its perceived historical relationship with China, India has diligently avoided establishing a formal relationship with Taiwan. However, notwithstanding India's stated commitment to OCP, the dynamics of the world order are changing in such a manner that the time has come for India to look at its relation with Taiwan more critically.

Over time India proceeded tentatively towards Taiwan, promoting only trade and investments yet ignoring formal diplomatic relations. India-Taiwan relations have substantial potential. Apprehensions on the government-to-government formal diplomatic ties are undermining the bilateral ties. Thereby the potential in various fields of partnership is underutilised. Therefore, internal dynamics can be maximised significantly through strengthening bilateral relations. India being a sovereign state, the national interest should be the absolute driving force rather than external consciousness. India needs to accept that China should not influence India's bilateral ties with Taiwan. The time has come to rethink India's commitments and preferences, particularly after the recent Galwan Valley dispute. Both the countries can benefit from the convergence of India's Act East policy and Taiwan's New Southbound Policy. This convergence can provide a precise framework to strengthen cooperation at several multidimensional levels from people to people to government level.

The evolution of QUAD can embrace Taiwan, and India can support Taiwan's participation in many multilateral dialogues, inter-party dialogues and diplomatic events. India can emulate the U.S. and Japan's policy towards Taiwan, prioritising Taiwan not only prevents Chinese influence but is beneficial economically, politically, and culturally to India.

Time has come for India to revisit its commitments to OCP after the recent Chinese aggression. India needs to engage with Taiwan through formal diplomatic ties. India needs to reconsider its stance of staying neutral in view of the potential benefits brought out earlier. Alternately, If India is still cautious about reviewing its stance on OCP then India should adopt more positive engagement through other channels with Taiwan, in order to derive the full benefit of bilateral ties for balancing its strategic interest.

Nevertheless, what prevails to conspicuous is how the two states continue the current momentum.

References

Basrur, R., & Shang-Su, W. (2021, May 6). CO21077 | Taiwan and India: Building Bigger To*gether? Retrieved October 2021, f*rom RSiS: https://www.rsis.edu.sg/rsis-publ*ication/rsis/taiwan-and*-india-building-bigger-together/#.YYypui8RrX8

Chaudhary, A., & Horton, C. (2020, October 20). India considers trade talks with Taiwan as both spa*r with China. Retrieved October 2021, from Business Standard: h*ttps://www.business-standard.com/article/current-affairs/india-considers-trade-talks-with-taiwan-as-both-spar-with-china-120102000533_1.html

Hashmi, S. (2020, January-March). India-Taiwan Relations: Time is Ripe to Bol*ster Ties. Indian Foreign Affairs Journal, 15(1),* 33-47.

Karackattu, J. T. (2019). The Case for a Pragmatic India-Taiwan *Parternship. New Delhi: Carnegie India.*

Pant, H. V. (2021, September 2). The strategic signal of an Indian presence in the South China Sea. Retrieved October 2021, from ORF: https://www.orfonline.org/research/strategic-sign*al-indian-presence-south-china-sea/*

Plus, T. (2021, September 6). Invest India/Taiwan Plus. Retrieved October 2021, from Invest India: https://www.investindia.gov.in/country/taiwan-plus

Press Trust of India, (2020, December 8). *Chinese exports to India decline 13%; India's trade up 16% in 2020.* Retrieved October 2021, from Busines Standard: https://www.business-standard.com/article/economy-policy/chinese-exports-to-india-decline-13-india-s-trade-up-16-in-2020-120120701335_1.html

9. Soldiers for Hire: Contextualising the Private Military's Legal Conundrums

Aman Sharma[1]

Abstract

The industry surrounding private military and security companies (PMSCs) is a conflict-driven industry. It often operates in regions with a significant security vacuum and a lack of an efficient legal and judicial system. This underscores the importance of effective regulatory oversight that may be international, national, or an amalgamation of both. Currently, the framing and subsequent enforcement of regulations continue to be a challenge due to divergent approaches among various stakeholders.The research paper focuses on the need to develop a consensus and bring accountability to the industry due to its far-reaching consequences. The research was based on analysing the existing regulations and using primary as well as secondary sources to identify legal gaps that impede the process of ensuring accountability from the PMSCs. Furthermore, the paper contextualised the legal ambiguities by taking up case studies of prominent PMSCs that have shaped current regulations.Apart from identifying the legal ambiguities, the research also highlighted the current scope of regulations and remedies in practice. It emphasised the importance of bringing good practises together and adding new dimensions to the definition of a mercenary by promoting better training procedures, effective and detailed vetting processes, and registering both PMSCs and individual contractors.

Key Words: Private Military and Security Companies, Accountability, Extraterritorial Jurisdiction, Huma Rights, DynCorp, Wagner Group, Blackwater, Montreux Document, ICoC

Introduction

The end of the 20th century saw a halt, albeit temporary, in rapid militarization around the globe. The median share of GDP allotted to military expenditure began to fall after the end of the Cold War. As a result, budgetary cuts and military down-

1 Aman Sharma is a student of MA Political Science from IGNOU.

sizing policies flooded the market with military hardware and human resources. Furthermore, neoliberal ideals motivated states to analyse the costs and benefits of the outsourcing model. Outsourcing of public services to the private sector was promoted, and security too became part of the phenomenon. The advent of neoliberal principles in the 1990s and the availability of skilled soldiers led to the corporatisation of the traditional mercenary industry.With security being viewed as a commodity of the service sector, the service providers came to be known as Private Military and Security Companies (PMSCs).

Role of PMSCs in International Conflict

PMSCs have seen significant growth since their evolution, with diversification in terms of both services and geography. Various conflicts around the globe have seen the use of PMSCs in active as well as passive roles, such as combat operations, strategic planning, intelligence collection, operational and logistical support, training, procurement, and maintenance. The combat teams of PMSCs are smaller in size, making them quicker to deploy, and the simplicity of their workflow allows for faster decision-making as compared to their conventional military counterparts. Due to the absence of political and bureaucratic intervention, the PMSCs are more adaptable to the conflict theatre as well. For instance, a curious example of the efficiency of PMSCs is Executive Outcomes (EO) and Specialised Tasks, Training, Equipment, and Protection (STTEP), which operated in Africa under Eeben Barlow. They used the strategy of "relentless pursuit" with quick mounted and dismounted manoeuvres and overwhelming firepower(Barlow, 2011). The conventional military was then tasked with consolidating the gains made by the shock troops and holding on to the area. Both STTEP and EO proved highly efficient in their operations but always faced fierce criticism, primarily due to their association with mining companies and the general anti-mercenary sentiments among many African nations. Both EO and STTEP were forced to withdraw from conflict because of international pressure and African conventions that were averse to contracting mercenaries. However, many African countries have shown a renewed interest in PMSCs and are exploring different avenues available in the marketplace.

This efficiency and availability of services of PMSCs is an asset for countries, particularly with weaker state military and institutions but powerful non-state actors such as rebel militias, terrorist organisations, drug cartels, and crime syndicates. Thus, they augment the state's capacity for security operations while reducing the requirement for the deployment of state military personnel. PMSC contractors are willing to serve for a longer period of time and have proved cheaper than the average expenditure incurred by the state for conventional soldiers. Contractors are also able to absorb the number of military casualties in comparison to the state, which is answerable to the people for the deaths of its military personnel. As Peter W. Singer noted for the Iraq war,(Singer, 2007)

"There was no outcry whenever contractors were called up and deployed, or even killed. If the gradual death toll among American troops threatened to slowly wear down public support, contractor casualties were not counted in official death tolls and had no impact on these ratings. These figures mean that the private military industry has suffered more losses in Iraq than the rest of the coalition of allied nations combined. The losses are also far more than any single U.S. Army division has experienced. "

Thus, PMSCs provide a low-cost solution to an otherwise complex security demand, and with an increasing number of intrastate and interstate conflicts, the demand for PMSCs is likely to grow. The expansion of PMSCs on a global level has also demonstrated a need for better regulations around the industry. These demands were made because an increasing number of companies were embroiled in several controversies that ranged from human rights violations to corruption in the conflict zone.

Legal Provisions Around PMSCs

Since the early 20th century, there have been laws that revolved around the use of mercenaries. These laws evolved over time, but remained insufficient to address the post-cold war version of so-called mercenaries. The ever-growing number of PMSCs, each with different functions, added several layers of complexity that became very difficult to address by generic internationalframework. These complexities further make it difficult to assign a particular definition to these entities. While there are entities that are legitimate business organisations that can be contracted for security services, there are also entities that work directly under the influence of the state to work as proxies in a conflict zone. If the former is termed as PMSC, the latter leans more towards the definition of mercenary. This spectrum, with its two ends as PMSCs and Mercenaries, creates many conceptual ambiguities, making it difficult to prosecute the offenders.

Deploying mercenaries began to be considered illegal in the 19th century, but only in the context of the impartiality of neutral nations. According to Article 4 of The Hague Conventions (1907), a neutral state had the obligation not to allow the formation of armed expeditions or to permit recruiting to be done on its territory. However, the convention did not mention the obligation to prevent people from crossing their borders to enlist in the armed forces of a belligerent. Also, it did not impose any prohibition on the use of mercenaries by warring nations. Similarly, the Third Geneva Convention (1949) also did not address the role of mercenaries directly. However, it provided them with prisoner of war status protections under

Article 4, but only if the individual, among other conditions, is accompanying the armed force of a party to the conflict. The first attempt to define the term "mercenaries" was undertaken by the Organisation of African Unity (OAU). This led to the constitution of the Ad Hoc Committee for Expulsions of Mercenaries (1967) and the Council of Ministers' committee of legal experts (1971) under the aegis of the OAU. The committees presented their reports to the OAU's council of ministers in 1972, which were later adopted as the Convention for the Elimination of Mercenarism in Africa at Libreville in 1977. Article 1 of the convention defines the term "mercenary" with a negative connotation. It stated that the objectives of a mercenary could include overthrowing a government of a member state of the OAU or obstructing the activities of a liberation movement. The article, however, did not mention any element of private gain or monetary compensation received by a mercenary for his activities. Initially, when in 1976, the Nigerian delegation introduced a proposal for an article to be inserted in Protocol 1 on International Armed Conflicts, no consensus could be reached. The prime reason for the impasse was the divergence of approach between the third world and the western states. The former being the ones that have to endure the activities of mercenaries and the latter being the ones supplying the manpower(France, 1992). Following further consideration and debate on the matter, the first additional protocol to the Geneva Convention (1977) was adopted and the legal obligations of mercenaries were defined.

Article 47(1) of the protocol prohibited the mercenaries from qualifying as lawful combatants or obtaining prisoner of war status. The article further laid out various conditions that a belligerent has to meet to be classified as a mercenary and be denied POW status. The conditions are of critical importance because they aim to differentiate between a mercenary and a volunteer. A person enlisted into service on a permanent or long-lasting basis in a foreign army as a result of an individual enlistment or through arrangements by their national authority is excluded from the category of mercenaries and can thus claim POW status. Some notable examples of such arrangements are the French Foreign Legion, the International Legion for the Defence of Ukraine (UKR Legion), and the now defunct MAVNI programme of the USA. Another element to be classified as a mercenary is the act of direct participation in hostilities. This leads to the exclusion of individuals classified as foreign advisers and military technicians as long as they do not participate in hostilities. One more important element is the incentive that motivates an individual to participate in a conflict. A mercenary is a person that is participating in hostilities for a desire of private gain and is offered material or monetary compensation in lieu of his combat services that is generally higher than similar ranks in the armed forces of the allied party to the conflict(France, 1992). This element was added to distinguish mercenaries from individuals that enlist solely for morals and ideals and get paid in accordance with the usual pay scale of other soldiers.

Apart from the Geneva conventions and other related frameworks, two major international initiatives, complementary to each other, were conceived. These were the Montreux document (2008) and the International Code of Conduct (2010), which were aimed at guiding the conduct of private military contractors. Currently, 58 states and 3 international organisations are signatories to the Montreux document, while the International Code of Conduct Association has hundreds of PMSCs as its members(Federal Department of Foreign Affairs of Switzerland, 2022).

Montreux Document (2008)

Although not legally binding, the Montreux documents contain a compilation of relevant international legal obligations and good practises to be followed by all the stakeholders involved in the industry. The Montreux document, conceptualised by the International Committee of the Red Cross and the Swiss government, outlines and addresses the practical aspects associated with contracting PMSCs. These practises can be implemented during an armed conflict, a post-conflict scenario, or during peacetime as well. The Montreux document is mainly divided into two sections. The first clarifies states' existing obligations under International Humanitarian Law while employing the services of PMSCs. It further divides the states into three categories: contracting, territorial, and home states, to define their obligations according to their respective assigned category. It goes on to list obligations such as protecting human rights, conducting investigations in cases of violations, and providing remedies to victims. The second section of the document consists of good practises for states related to PMSC regulation. It includes guidance on procedures, systems, and processes for contracting, licensing, and approving PMSCs to operate in a state. The guidance also includes recommendations on establishing effective monitoring mechanisms(The Montreux Document).

International Code of Conduct (2013)

After the creation of the Montreux document, PMSC too needed to be involved in the process. This led to another major initiative known as the International Code of Conduct (ICoC) for private security service providers. It is a multi-stakeholder led initiative, including the PMSCs, states, human rights organisations, academicians, and industry clients. Its aim is to translate the existing rules into principles for the PMSCs to implement during their operations. It outlines rules and principles regarding human rights, use of force, detention, and the prohibition of torture and human trafficking. It also prescribes policies for the management, such as vetting, training, weapons handling, and grievance procedures. The ICoC further requires the PMSCs to comply with these corporate good practises in their contracts for personnel, subcontractors, and clients(ICOCA, n.d.).

Case Studies

As stated by Max Weber, the concept of monopoly of violence meant a legitimate state had the right to authorise the use of force. Although historically true, the concept has been facing challenges in contemporary times with the emergence of several non-state actors. The erosion of state sovereignty due to globalisation and the outbreak of ethnic conflicts and proxy wars around the globe has led to the weakening of the idea of the state's monopoly over violence. The vacuum thus created was filled by PMSCs in a varied number of ways depending on the concerned scenarios. Although there have been several initiatives to regulate the industry, as mentioned above, the issue is the lack of convergence between international and national law on the one hand, and government regulation and industry self-regulation on the other.

There are three case studies mentioned below that illustrate different historical scenarios that developed in private military contractors' space across different parts of the world. Through the case studies, the paper attempts to contextualise the role of PMSCs in different types of conflict zones and the legal aspects (both national and transnational) associated with their role.

Study 1: Blackwater in Iraq and its role as a protective service provider for high-value individuals as well as logistics.

Study 2: Wagner in Africa as an extended arm of Russian influence in the continent.

Study 3: DynCorp in Bosnia for Law Enforcement Duties in Collaboration with the UN.

1. Blackwater

Following the invasion of Iraq in 2003, the number of military personnel deployed in the country decreased, while the number of for-hire personnel increased to around 1,60,000 by 2007. Multiple companies operating in the region hired Blackwater and other similar groups, nearing 181 in number, for jobs such as securing logistic routes or escorting highly valued individuals. Since the companies were for-profit and not aligned with the strategic objectives of the US, the contractors often carried out tasks that were to the detriment of the "Winning Hearts and Minds" strategy of the US Military(Singer, 2007).

After the Vietnam War, military leaders in the US wanted a policy to preserve the ties between the national foreign policy objectives and the will of the population at home. This gave birth to the 'Abrams Doctrine'. The doctrine's objective was to solve the problem of the mobilisation of reserve forces, which was missing during the Vietnam War. This type of mobilisation was intended to link the reserve forces to the national will for war, allowing the military to be held accountable to the people.

During the 2003 invasion of Iraq, the problem of insufficient forces needed a full-scale mobilisation of the national guard and reserves at home. This could have prompted a massive public outcry against the invasion. Employing the private military industry to fill this gap was the answer to many of the problems faced by the leaders in the executive branch. The PMSCs offered the role of reserve forces and carried out secondary duties without any political blowback at home. PMSC casualties were seldom part of the news cycle in the US and were mostly treated as expendable.

But an unintended consequence was the misalignment of objectives between the contractors and the conventional military. The outsourcing business slowly turned the logistics and operations into a for-profit endeavour with the establishment of ever expanding "green zones" and lavish military bases. Bigger bases yielded more money for the stockholders but also disconnected the forces from the local populace. A dynamic and active supply chain of resources to run these bases meant more and more convoys plying to and fro on the Iraqi roads. This made the contractors one of the most hated aspects of the USA's military occupation of Iraq.

Blackwater in particular, had a notorious reputation among the Iraqi population due to their highly visible role in escorting American officials. The firm was often accused of incidents of unruly behaviour. One such incident of alleged mistaken identity escalated to the infamous Nisour Square massacre in 2007 at the hands of Blackwater employees during escort duty. Prior to this major incident, there were numerous reported instances of abuse and unprofessional behaviour by contractors on Iraqi streets as well as in the detention centres. It was reported that 100% of the translators and up to 50% of the interrogators at Abu Ghraib Prison were private contractors from the firms Titan and CACI. The US Army found that contractors were involved in 36% of the proven abuse incidents from 2003–2004. However, while US Army soldiers involved in the Abu Ghraib abuse were court martialled, contractors and their firms still haven't been charged, prosecuted, or punished(Singer, 2004).

The agreement under which the contractors were working in Iraq explicitly mentioned at that time that the Iraqi government didn't have jurisdiction over the contractors. This made it impossible for the Iraqi government to prosecute Blackwater employees. Under the Military Extraterritorial Jurisdiction Act (MEJA), 2000, the US federal government was granted the authority to prosecute private military contractors for overseas crime. But since the employees were under contract by the state department and not the department of defence, it was unclear whether the law was applicable to them. Regardless, the Department of Justice pursued the case, and the contractors were found guilty of manslaughter in 2014(US Department of Justice, 2019). After the Nisour Square shootings, the House of Representatives passed the MEJA Expansion and Enforcement Act of 2007 ("MEJA Expansion Act"), which would have extended the reach of MEJA to all contractors "in an area, or in close proximity to an area (as designated by the Department of Defence), where the Armed Forces are conducting a contingency operation." But the Senate failed to act on the bill, which led to its failure to become law.

But implementing MEJA in a conflict zone also has several issues. Peter W. Singer stated(Singer, 2007),

"The reality is that no US Attorney likes to waste limited budgets on such messy, complex cases 9,000 miles outside their district, even if they were fortunate enough to have the evidence at hand"

Currently, alongside MEJA, the conduct of contractors is also guided by the Uniform Code of Military Justice (UCMJ), whose jurisdiction was extended to military contractors in 2007. However, the UCMJ trial can almost certainly be challenged on constitutional grounds, and its effective implementation will be dependent on how it is interpreted in different scenarios and the government's intent to prosecute.

2. Wagner Group

According to Russian law, private military contractors are illegal and unconstitutional. After a series of debates in the Duma, the state reaffirmed the illegality in March 2018. But there are exceptions, such as Rosneft and Gazprom, the Russian state-controlled oil and gas companies, which are allowed to employ private security guards to guard their assets and are authorised to detain or kill suspects and intruders. Despite the ban on mercenary activities mentioned in Chapter 34, Article 359 of the Criminal Code of the Russian Federation, many private military contractors have flourished over time, like the RSB-Group and Moran Security Group, which are more comparable to their western counterparts. These groups do maintain their connections with the state but mostly operate on a commercial basis.

Expressing his support for PMSCs, Putin said that such firms are an instrument for realising national interests without direct participation of the state(Sysoev, 2012). There have been multiple attempts and proposals in the Russian Duma to legalise PMSCs, but none has made progress. This lack of legal status has an important upside to it. It serves as a convenient tool for the Russian federation for plausible deniability against any covert or risky actions of the groups. Illegality also serves the purpose of effective control over the activities of the groups, as disloyalty to the power centre would result in legal action. The market restrictions caused due to illegality also allow only the favourites to accrue profits from the industry and allow prosecution of outsiders. The incident involving the arrest and subsequent prosecution of mercenaries of Slavonic Corps in 2014 could be an example of one such case.

Russian PMSC activity picked up during and after the Crimean crisis, with its subsequent global expansion into Eastern Europe, the Middle East, and Africa. The group that took prominence was the Wagner Group, which first went into action during Russia's annexation of Crimea. The "little green men" that occupied the key strategic locations in Crimea in 2014 had some Wagner elements, along with Russian SOF and Spetsnaz GRU units, within them. They later moved on to support the pro-Russian separatist groups in the Donbas region.

There have been several investigations that allege that Russia's intelligence agency, the GRU, secretly funds and oversees the operation of the Wagner group, with its founder being Dmitri Utkin, a former Russian army officer. The group has also been linked to Yevgeny Prigozhin, a Russian oligarch very close to Putin. Prigozhin is also known for financing the Internet Research Agency (IRA), a troll farm involved in spreading disinformation campaigns on social media (U.S. Department of the Treasury, 2020). Several IRA-related troll accounts have been taken down by Meta and Twitter for suspicious activities around the globe, including Africa (Gleicher, 2020). In the months leading up to the 2021 Coup in Mali, a coordinated network of Facebook pages promoted pro-Russian and anti-French narratives to mobilise public support for the deployment of the Wagner Group. Similarly, before the January, 2022, coup in Burkina Faso, a network of Facebook pages was propped up to advocate for a wider revolution in the Sahel region and project Russia as a crucial partner and an alternative to France.

The group and its associated operations serve as a major foreign policy tool for the Russian state with the aim of creating African dependencies on Moscow's security apparatus to access African resources. They operate through a web of shell companies, carrying out a broad spectrum of Kremlin-backed operations across the Middle East and Africa. In return for COIN and security operations, Russia seeks payments in the form of concessions for natural resources, substantial commercial contracts, or access to strategic locations, such as airbases or ports. For instance, Wagner deployed its operatives in Sudan to quell local uprisings against Omar al-Bashir's government. As payment, a company by the name Meroe Gold was granted exclusive mining rights for gold in Sudan, which is a subsidiary of M-Invest, which itself is a subsidiary of M-Finance, founded by Prigozhin. Bashir was also in talks with Moscow to set up a naval base on the eastern coast of Sudan in 2019, a proposal still being considered by Khartoum(Fasanotti, 2022).

In 2015, the group started operating in Syria, alongside the pro-government forces in direct combat as well as defensive operations to secure oilfields. In Libya, the group has been operating since 2016, in support of forces loyal to General KhalifaHaftar. Apart from active combat services, the Wagner Group is also involved in securing mining operations of precious minerals like gold, diamonds, and uranium. The group was invited to the Central African Republic and Sudan to guard diamond and gold mines, respectively. The US treasury department has also alleged that the presence of the group in Africa is a cover to provide protection to Prigozhin's mining companies, such as M Invest and Lobaye Invest. The group was invited to participate in the offensive against Islamic militant groups in West Africa, which ultimately led to the pull-out of French forces from Mali in 2021.

Wagner's expansion into Africa and the Middle East provides much-needed space for Moscow to pursue a dynamic and aggressive foreign policy in order to counter the influence of its western counterparts The Kremlin is neither a signatory to the Montreux Document nor a member of the International Code for Conduct of Private Security Providers' Association. Unlike most other PMSCs, Wagner isn't a true commercial entity operating in a global marketplace and is not a legally registered entity in Russia. An officially designated operational structure does not exist and the key people, state or non-state, financing and operating the entity do not admit to their roles. Apart from nationalism, the salaries, substantially higher than the average Russian wage, remain a huge incentive for fighters to join the group.

3. DynCorp International

The success of the outsourcing model and the associated legal and regulatory frameworks put into effect have resulted in the diversification of the industry and the creation of several local PMSCs in different countries. This also led to several terminations, mergers, and acquisitions of PMSCs to increase their scope and scale of operations. For instance, Amentum, a former AECOM management service unit, was acquired by private equity firms American Securities and Lindsay Goldberg for $2.4 billion in February 2020. Eight months later, Amentum completed the acquisition of another company called DynCorp International, resulting in a net revenue of at least $6 billion and approximately 34,000 employees in nearly 30 countries(Wilkers, 2020). DynCorp, founded in 1946, was one of the largest government services firms in the US. Apart from providing security, it had bagged contracts for air operations, both combat and non-combat, aviation maintenance, contingency operation support, intelligence gathering, and training. It had provided its services to the US military in multiple theatres, including Iraq, Angola, Somalia, Bolivia, Colombia, Kosovo, and Kuwait.

The company was a significant player in the industry, and since its inception, it had bagged several contracts in almost every financial year. It was even responsible for providing security to former Afghan President Hamid Karzai's presidential guard and had trained most of the police forces in Afghanistan. The US Congress constituted an auditing agency named the Special Inspector General for Afghanistan to oversee government spending during the US presence in the region. According to a SIGAR report in the year 2014, DynCorp received a total of $2.8 billion in contracts, approximately 69% of the State Department's contracts for reconstruction work in Afghanistan (Siegel, 2017). The majority of contracts were earmarked for governance and rule of law activities like training the Afghan National Police, establishing the related infrastructure, and fielding police equipment and vehicles. As a private entity, the company has all the rights to compete for government contracts, but a well-documented history of scandals makes it a peculiar case in point.

A diplomatic cable leaked by WikiLeaks documented a conversation between the former Minister of Interior (MOI) HanifAtmar and Assistant US Ambassador, Joseph A. Mussomeli, in 2009. The conversation was an attempt by the MOI to suppress news of DynCorp contractors hiring underage 'Dancing Boys', an Afghan tradition named "BachaBazi," which borders on child abuse(Boone, 2010). Although DynCorp terminated the accused employees and repatriated them back, no criminal action was taken against them in the US. This wasn't the first instance where contractors were involved in sex abuse-related crimes. The most prominent case was the Bosnia Scandal, which was discovered in the late 1990s.

In 1995, a UN mission was established in Bosnia and Herzegovina following the signing of the Dayton Accords. As a result, an international police task force was setup in the country to train and officiate law enforcement duties. When the sex trafficking scandal was unearthed in Bosnia, it was alleged that several IPTF officials and US military contractors from DynCorp were involved in the trafficking of women and collaborated with the international syndicate. Many victims identified IPTF and DynCorp employees as being involved in sexual abuse by visiting brothels, purchasing slaves, and reselling them.

DynCorp issued a statement in January 2002 stating that "The corporation took prompt action to understand and deal with the situation, including the termination of contracts of individuals found to be involved in improper behaviour"(Human Rights Watch, 2002).

The contracts between the UN and the countries providing police officers state that member states, not local courts, are expected to initiate appropriate disciplinary or legal (civil or penal) action. The employees involved, including eight Americans, were repatriated back to their home countries. While NATO and other concerned authorities refused to waive the immunity of the contractors, the practise of quick repatriation severely hampered local investigations. The U.S. Department of Defence confirmed to Human Rights Watch that no cases had been prosecuted under the Military Extraterritorial Jurisdiction Act as of October 2002 due to the failure to issue regulations implementing the law. DynCorp also confirmed that none of its own contractors faced prosecution:

"The company at all times cooperated with the authorities in investigating these matters…To our knowledge, no criminal action was instituted by either the U.S. Army or authorities in either country with respect to the activities of the individuals"(Human Rights Watch, 2002).

Ben Johnston, a former employee at DynCorp, stated under oath that DynCorp employees continued to purchase women. He also alleged that although some employees faced repatriation, there was nothing said at work about anything they couldn't do, so it just continued(Human Rights Watch, 2002).

Contemporary Legal Gaps in the Context of PMSCs Analysed in the Case Studies

PMSCs have the potential to severely alter the dynamics of a conflict. On one hand, they can be effective in combating a threat that grows beyond a state's capacity, as seen in the case of EO and then STTEP.On the other hand, it can give rise to cases of serious violations of rights in an unregulated security environment, as seen in the cases of Blackwater, Wagner, and DynCorp. Although there are several international conventions and regulations surrounding PMSCs, their non-binding and ambiguous nature give rise to legal vacuums. The absence of a comprehensive framework and an effective oversight body allows PMSCs to gain a monopoly over the security situation in a conflict region. As evident in the case studies, over the years, there have been attempts to exploit these gaps for the vested interests of the parties involved, while attempts to address these gaps have also been taken up at both national and international level.

But it is important to note that the transnational nature of PMSCs requires a multi-government and multi-stakeholder approach to develop a consensus. Both the Montreux document and the ICoC were aimed at solving this issue. The main objectives of the Montreux document were to encourage states to conduct effective due diligence while contacting PMSCs and further encourage PMSCs to conduct proper vetting of the individual contractors. The International Code of Conduct Association (ICoCA), an association of PMSCs, established an International Code of Conduct (ICoC) to ensure that signatories respect IHL. However, the non-binding nature of both of these documents results in the contractors' professional debarment rather than conviction in court. The key challenge here is the lack of national will and capacity to implement existing norms at the national level. This is because the nature and work of the PMSCs often benefits the larger geopolitical interests of the governments employing them. This, according to the United Nations working group on mercenaries, becomes an impediment for effective implementation of multilateral treaties(OHCHR, 2018). For instance, the UN international convention against the recruitment, use, financing, and training of mercenaries has not been signed by any of the five permanent UN security council members, i.e., the United States, France, Russia, China, and the United Kingdom.

In the 21st century, traditional mercenaries have become less and less common. Rather than being involved in direct combat operations, most PMSCs nowadays have transformed into security companies involved mainly in defensive and support roles. Hence, there is a need to develop consistent terminologies and definitions for different elements involved in the PMSC sector. The overly restrictive existing definitions have led to few possibilities for prosecuting perpetrators involved in human rights violations and other crimes in a conflict zone. These gaps that have emerged during the contemporary conflicts make it imperative to distinguish between contractors, volunteers, foreign fighters, and terrorists. These actors often have overlapping objectives and motivations for taking part in combat. Hence, the definition should go beyond the scope of human rights violations and armed conflicts. The role of mercenaries and PMSC contractors in criminal activities such as smuggling weapons and drugs, human trafficking, and illegal mining needs to be analysed and taken into consideration to develop a more nuanced definition.

In the early 1990s and 2000s, the human rights violations involving Blackwater and DynCorp sparked a heated debate about closing regulatory gaps and punishing perpetrators of violence against civilians. Following that, several domestic and international policy and legal challenges were addressed. As a result, currently, accountability for PMSCs is available through administrative sanctions, but there is still a lack of emphasis on penal actions and enforceable remedies for victims. A consensus must be reached in order to hold the involved PMSC liable for compensation to the victim of abuse. Remedies in line with the Alien Torture Statue (ATS) of the US can be developed to prosecute contractors in their home state. ATS allows foreign nationals to seek remedies in US courts for human rights violations committed outside the United States, but there needs to be a sufficient connection to the country. ATS was used in the case of Abu Ghraib prison abuse as well as in the lawsuit Al Shimari, et al. v. CACI, currently active in US court(Al Shimari, et al. v. CACI, 2008).

States should ensure that their domestic criminal laws extend beyond their borders to prosecute their nationals and locally-based companies for serious crimes abroad. But this is only possible if other agreements and contractual obligations do not impede the judicial process. CACI, in 2019, argued that it should be protected under the legal doctrine of "Derivative Sovereign Immunity" during the trials of the Abu Ghraib Prison case but was denied any respite by the courts(Al Shimari, et al. v. CACI, 2019). Also, in the case of Blackwater, MEJA was extended to prosecute contractors, and the Justice Department was successful in convictions(US Department of Justice, 2008). But on the other hand, in the absence of an efficient judicial system in the area of operation, extraterritorial investigations are challenging. These challenges then result in cases ending up in plea agreements rather than going to trials, which is what happened in AL-Quraishi v. L-3, the Abu Ghraib prison case(Al-Quraishi, et al. v. Nakhla and L-3 Services, 2012). Assigning this responsibility of oversight to the national military with which the contractors are embedded can solve this issue to some extent.

There are also discrepancies among different countries over regulations on the use of force and firearms by PMSCs. In Nigeria, STTEP was able to bypass sanctions on the country to acquire weapons and armoured vehicles. This is because there are no distinct provisions on illegal acquisition of weapons and on illicit trafficking in arms by PMSCs. The PMSCs should adhere to the international standards related to arms control licensing procedures, arms transfer, acquisition of weapons, and trafficking in arms. It is essential to establish some standard procedures for acquiring, exporting, importing, and possessing weapons by PMSCs.

Another impediment that still plagues PMSC regulations is ensuring effective compliance from several countries if they aim to use PMSCs as extended arms of state influence, as in the case of Russia and China. But unlike Russia, China allows the operation of security companies in an indirect role while banning them from direct combat roles. Among the 7000 security companies active in China, the most significant player in the sector is Frontier Service Group (FSB). A company founded by Erik Prince, the founder of Blackwater, is currently undertaking several major projects linked to the Belt and Road Initiative of China. Interestingly, FSB was founded in the year 2014 as a company that provides logistical, aviation, and security services, which coincided with the Chinese push for BRI. While Prince resigned from the positions of executive director and chairman in 2021, CITIC Group, a Chinese state-owned conglomerate, continues to be one of the major shareholders of the company(Lam, 2018). Although there have been instances of FSB being linked to or providing facilities to some suspicious clients, there haven't been any cases reported so far that link FSB to human rights violations.

The Wagner group, now widely active in Africa and Ukraine, comes closest to a traditional mercenary group. There were reports of significant human rights abuses by Wagner mercenaries in its areas of operation, the most recent one being the Central African Republic. Like the US, the EU also sanctioned individuals and entities linked to the Wagner group, but holding them accountable is incredibly difficult as they operate either in an unregulated conflict zone or in consonance with the ruling leaders of the host state. Since the contracts of Wagner are often directed and guided by Russian state interests, it is highly unlikely it would be prosecuted for its actions both at home and in the host state. This underscores the importance of the rule of attribution as guided by the Articles on State Responsibility, 2001 (ASR), used to hold a state accountable for internationally wrongful acts. A similar direction has been pursued by the Montreux document to identify the home state of a PMSC. Thus, the principle of command responsibility may be invoked to maintain accountability(Maddocks, 2021).

Conclusion

International humanitarian law does not prohibit the use of PMSCs and mercenaries during armed conflict. Although a state that has ratified one or both of the conventions—the 1977 Organization of African Unity Convention for the Elimination of Mercenarism in Africa and the 1989 International Convention against the Recruitment, Use, Financing, and Training of Mercenaries—is required to prosecute and punish mercenaries. Furthermore, the definition of mercenaries in Article 47 of Additional Protocol 1, being restrictive in nature, does not cover PMSCs under its ambit. Thus, PMSCs are considered civilians. They are prohibited from participating in hostilities and are not entitled to combatant or POW status if captured. However, being civilians, they are accorded adequate rights under the Fourth Geneva Convention(Redaelli, 2021).Despite ambiguities, PMSCs come under the ambit of the Geneva Conventions in one way or another, but the lack of clarity over the subject often leads to exploitation of these ambiguities for vested interests by states, corporations, or individual contractors.

While the Montreux document and the ICoC continue to be the best available options for PMSC regulation, they reinforce the viewpoint that PMSCs should be regulated and not outright banned. Further, there is a divergence of views over the extent of regulations as well. Many national governments and industry stakeholders, as well as the Swiss initiatives, prescribe a more lenient approach that includes self-regulation. On the other hand, the UN advocates a more statist, hard-law position on regulating the PMSCs (Prem, 2021).It is imperative to converge the two approaches to create an all-inclusive framework that addresses, apart from international legal gaps, shortcomings in domestic regulations as well. The major challenge that remains in achieving this convergence of viewpoints is striking a balance between a state's national interest and humanitarian responsibility on the one hand and industry aspirations on the other that lean towards self-regulation.

Beyond the provisions and gaps that are mentioned in this paper, there exist a wide variety of codes of conduct, good practices, and national legislation that are worthy of further exploration. An ever-expanding network of institutions, voluntary practices, rules, and regulations always gives way to ambiguities. Instead, these can be integrated and studied to develop a more comprehensive framework for

PMSCs. This may include, among other things, a better definition, a ban on certain activities, registration with national authorities, and licensing of PMSC activities abroad while establishing an oversight and judicial mechanism to investigate and prosecute human rights violations.

References

Al Shimari, et al. v. CACI, 08-cv-0827 GBL-JFA (United States District Court for the Eastern District of Virginia September 15, 2008). Retrieved September 7, 2022, from https://ccrjustice.org/sites/default/files/assets/Amended%20Complaint%20on%20the%20Defendants.pdf

Al Shimari, et al. v. CACI, 1:08-cv-0827 LMB-JFA (United States District Court for the Eastern District of Virginia Febraury 28, 2019). Retrieved September 7, 2022, from Business & Human Rights Resource Centre: https://ccrjustice.org/sites/default/files/attach/2019/03/1150_2-28-19_CACI%20memo%20MTD%20derivative%20immunity%20web.pdf

Al-Quraishi, et al. v. Nakhla and L-3 Services, 8:08-cv-01696-PJM (United States District Court for the District of Maryland, Greenbelt division October 10, 2012). Retrieved September 7, 2022, from https://ccrjustice.org/sites/default/files/assets/133_2012-10-10%20Al-Quraishi_Marginal%20Order%20approving%20Notice%20of%20Voluntary%20Dismissal.pdf

Archibong, E. J. (2021, July 21). Private Military Contractors: Legitimate Entrepreneurs or New Fashioned Mercenaries. Journal of Civil & Legal Sciences, 10(7). doi:10.4172/2169-0170.1000279

Arnpriester, N. (2017). Combating Impunity: The Private Military Industry, Human Rights, and the "Legal Gap". University of Pennsylvania Journal of International Law, 38(4). Retrieved August 25, 2022, from https://scholarship.law.upenn.edu/jil/vol38/iss4/3/

Article 359, Mercenarism. (1996). The Criminal Code Of The Russian Federation. Retrieved December 15, 2022, from http://www.russian-criminal-code.com/PartII/SectionXII/Chapter34.html

Barlow, E. (2011, August 21). Relentless pursuit: A neglected COIN principle? Retrieved September 22, 2022, from Eeben Barlow's military and security blog: http://eebenbarlowsmilitaryandsecurityblog.blogspot.com/2011/08/relentless-pursuit-neglected-coin.html

Bodurtha, M. (2022, April 1). An Obligation to Regulate: How Private Military Companies Embolden Conflict with Impunity from the Middle East to Central Africa. Columbia Journal of Transnational Law. Retrieved September 15, 2022, from https://www.jtl.columbia.edu/bulletin-blog/an-obligation-to-regulate-how-private-military-companies-embolden-conflict-with-impunity-from-the-middle-east-to-central-africa

Boone, J. (2010, December 2). Foreign contractors hired Afghan 'dancing boys', WikiLeaks cable reveals. Retrieved September 15, 2022, from The Gaurdian: https://www.

theguardian.com/world/2010/dec/02/foreign-contractors-hired-dancing-boys

Faite, A. (2004, October 15). Involvement of Private Contractors in Armed Conflict: Implications under International Humanitarian Law. Defence Studies, 4(2). Retrieved from https://www.icrc.org/en/doc/resources/documents/article/other/pmc-article-310804.htm

Fasanotti, F. S. (2022, February 8). Russia's Wagner Group in Africa: Influence, commercial concessions, rights violations, and counterinsurgency failure. Retrieved August 15, 2022, from Brookings: https://www.brookings.edu/blog/order-from-chaos/2022/02/08/russias-wagner-group-in-africa-influence-commercial-concessions-rights-violations-and-counterinsurgency-failure/

Federal Department of Foreign Affairs of Switzerland. (2022). Participating States of the Montreux Document. Retrieved September 15, 2022, from Federal Department of Foreign Affairs FDFA: https://www.eda.admin.ch/eda/en/fdfa/foreign-policy/international-law/international-humanitarian-law/private-military-security-companies/participating-states.html

France, M. (1992). Mercenaries and International Law. Georgia Journal of International & Comparative Law, 22(1), 103-150. Retrieved August 22, 2022, from https://digitalcommons.law.uga.edu/gjicl/vol22/iss1/5/

Gleicher, N. (2020, October 8). Removing Coordinated Inauthentic Behavior. Retrieved August 22, 2022, from Meta: https://about.fb.com/news/2020/10/removing-coordinated-inauthentic-behavior-september-report/

Gwatiwa, T. T. (2016, December 1). Private Military and Security Companies policy in Africa: Regional policy stasis as Agency in international politics. Scientia Militaria - South African Journal of Military Studies, 68-81. doi:10.5787/44-2-1176

Hammes, T. X. (2010). Private Contractors in Conflict Zones: The Good, the Bad, and the Strategic Impact. Institute for National Strategic Studies, Center for Strategic. National Defense University Press. Retrieved August 15, 2022, from https://apps.dtic.mil/sti/citations/ADA536906

Human Rights Watch. (2002). Hopes betrayed: Trafficking of women and girls to post-conflict Bosnia and Herzegovina for forced prostitution. Human Rights Watch. Retrieved September 14, 2022, from https://www.hrw.org/legacy/reports/2002/bosnia/Bosnia1102-01.htm#P164_4470

ICOCA. (n.d.). The code. Retrieved August 15, 2022, from ICOCA: https://icoca.ch/the-code/

Lam, A. (2018, March 7). CITIC-Group-Increases-Stake-In-HK-Listed-Frontier-Services-Group-To-40.51. Retrieved September 15, 2022, from Nikkei Asia: https://asia.nikkei.com/NAR/Articles/CITIC-Group-Increases-Stake-In-HK-Listed-Frontier-Services-Group-To-40.51

Maddocks, J. (2021, April 28). Russia, The Wagner Group, And The Issue Of Attribution. Retrieved September 15, 2022, from Articles of War: https://lieber.westpoint.edu/russia-wagner-group-attribution/

Markusen, M. (2022, January 12). A Stealth Industry: The Quiet Expansion of Chinese Private Security Companies. Retrieved September 15, 2022, from CSIS: https://www.csis.org/analysis/stealth-industry-quiet-expansion-chinese-private-security-companies

Mquirmi, N. E. (2022). Private military and security companies: a new form of mercenarism? Policy Center for the New South. Retrieved September 15, 2022, from https://www.policycenter.ma/publications/private-military-and-security-companies-new-form-mercenarism

Nimkar, R. (2009). From Bosnia to Baghdad the case for regulating Private Military and Security Companies. Journal of Public and International Affairs - Princeton University. Retrieved September 22, 2022, from https://jpia.princeton.edu/sites/g/files/toruqf1661/files/2009-1.pdf

OHCHR. (2018, April). OHCHR. Retrieved September 14, 2022, from Working Group on the use of mercenaries: https://www.ohchr.org/sites/default/files/MercenarismandPrivateMilitarySecurityCompanies.pdf

Prem, B. (2021). The regulation of private military and security companies: Analyzing power in multi-stakeholder initiatives. In Contemporary Security Policy. Contemporary Security Policy, 345–370. doi:10.1080/13523260.2021.1897225

Redaelli, C. (2021, November 9). The Involvement of Mercenaries and Private Military Security Companies in Armed Conflicts: What Does IHL Say? (G. Academy, Interviewer) Retrieved September 22, 2022, from Geneva Academy: https://www.geneva-academy.ch/news/detail/482-the-involvement-of-mercenaries-and-private-military-security-companies-in-armed-conflicts-what-does-ihl-say

Siegel, J. (2017, July 12). The Real Winner of the Afghan War Is This Shady Military Contractor. Retrieved August 12, 2022, from The daily Beast: https://www.thedailybeast.com/the-real-winner-of-the-afghan-war-is-this-shady-military-contractor

Singer, P. W. (2004). The private military industry and Iraq: What have we learned and where to next? Geneva Centre for the Democratic Control of Armed Forces (DCAF). Retrieved September 22, 2022, from https://www.files.ethz.ch/isn/14132/pp4_singer.pdf

Singer, P. W. (2007). Can't Win With 'Em, Can't Go To War Without 'Em: Private Military Contractors and Counterinsurgency. The Brookings Institution. brookings.edu. Retrieved August 15, 2022, from Brookings: https://www.brookings.edu/research/cant-win-with-em-cant-go-to-war-without-em-private-military-contractors-and-counterinsurgency/

Singer, P. W. (2007, October 2). The Dark Truth about Blackwater. Retrieved August 22, 2022, from Brookings: https://www.brookings.edu/articles/the-dark-truth-about-blackwater/

Singer, P. W. (2007, January 4). The Law Catches Up to Private Militaries, Embeds. Retrieved August 22, 2022, from Brookings: https://www.brookings.edu/articles/the-law-catches-up-to-private-militaries-embeds/

Sopko, John F. (2014). Department of state assistance to Afghanistan. Office of Special Inspector General for Afghanistan Reconstruction. Retrieved August 15, 2022, from https://www.sigar.mil/pdf/special%20projects/SIGAR-14-49-SP.pdf

Sysoev, G. (2012, April 11). Putin supported the idea of creating private military companies in Russia. Retrieved September 22, 2022, from RIA Novosti: https://ria.ru/20120411/623227984.html

The Montreux Document. (n.d.). Retrieved August 15, 2022, from Federal Department of Foreign Affairs FDFA: https://www.eda.admin.ch/eda/en/home/foreign-policy/international-law/international-humanitarian-law/private-military-security-companies/montreux-document.html

U.S. Department of the Treasury. (2020, July 15). Treasury Targets Financier's Illicit Sanctions Evasion Activity. Retrieved August 15, 2022, from U.S. Department of the Treasury: https://home.treasury.gov/news/press-releases/sm1058

US Department of Justice. (2008, December 8). Five Blackwater Employees Indicted on Manslaughter and Weapons Charges for Fatal Nisur Square Shooting in Iraq. Retrieved September 7, 2022, from US Department of Justice: https://www.justice.gov/archive/opa/pr/2008/December/08-nsd-1068.html

US Department of Justice. (2019, August 14). Former Blackwater Employee Sentenced to Life Imprisonment for Murder in 2007 Shooting at Nisur Square in Iraq. Retrieved August 15, 2022, from https://www.justice.gov/: https://www.justice.gov/usao-dc/pr/former-blackwater-employee-sentenced-life-imprisonment-murder-2007-shooting-nisur-square

Wilkers, R. (2020, September 25). Amentum hits gas pedal with DynCorp acquisition. Retrieved September 22, 2022, from Washington Technology: https://washingtontechnology.com/2020/09/amentum-hits-gas-pedal-with-dyncorp-acquisition/355028/

Wilson, G. (2016, April 5). PROXY Capabilities – The History and Future of Russian Private Military Companies. Retrieved September 22, 2022, from Strifeblog: https://www.strifeblog.org/2016/04/05/the-history-and-future-of-russian-private-military-companies/#_ednref2

10. Russia, India, and China Alliance – Towards balancing the World Order

Ridipt Singh[1]

Abstract

The global financial order that emerged after the Second World War was primarily western-led with the USA as the center essentially making the international state system a unipolar one. The need for reforms in the global financial order has long been discussed citing the dangers of globalization that became evident after the 2008 global financial crisis and more recently after the Russian invasion of Ukraine in 2022. In response to the sanction being imposed, Russia has taken up initiatives to detach itself from the dollar-based global financial order where China and India are seen as potential partners. The research paper takes up the concept of the Primakov Doctrine and the current Russia-India China (RIC) trilateral as a possible strategic triangle that can counterbalance the western-led global financial order by adopting a common currency.

The study covers the origins of the Primakov Doctrine, the geopolitical dynamics of the past, and possible reasons for its failure in the initial stages. Further, the research focuses on the current RIC format, its limitations, and how it can be transformed into a strategic alliance. The case of the de-dollarization effort is used to argue that it can be a common vision that the three countries can pursue which would act as the foundation for turning the current RIC into a strategic alliance. Taking examples of multilateral platforms like BRICS and SCO, the paper includes the relevance of RIC in the contemporary era in addition to the complications that India is likely to face given its ties with the USA, membership in the Quad, and the possibility of the RIC being perceived as an anti-west coalition.

Using an empirical research approach with qualitative methods using information that is publicly available from secondary sources like academic literature, research articles, and official statements from the government, the research paper addresses the subsequent questions regarding the possibility of the formation of such an alliance and its feasibility. These questions include how can India and China become part of an alliance amidst border disputes, do Russia, India, and China qual

1 Ridipt Singh is a final year student of MA International Studies at Symbiosis School of International Studies, Symbiosis International University, Pune, India.

ify as an Optimum Currency Area or whether cooperation is possible without a common currency,what makes the contemporary era conducive for pursuing such economic framework and what implications such developments will have in the context of the Indo-Pacific.

The paper provides policy recommendations based on case studies from other cooperating states and organizations regarding how a monetary union can be formed despite strained relations among states and the required preconditions to make such an initiative successful.

Key Words: Primakov Doctrine, India, Russia, China, De-Dollarization, Common Currency, BRICS, SCO.

Introduction

The idea of India, Russia, and China forming a strategic trilateral was first conceptualized by Yevgeni Primakov in 1998 during his visit to India.This idea later came to be known as the Primakov Doctrine. Russian Foreign Minister Sergey Lavrov stated, "the moment Yevgeny Primakov took charge, the Russian Foreign Ministry heralded a fundamental turn in foreign policy" (Denisov, 2017). The idea was a product of the geopolitical dynamics of the time. The post-Cold War era was marked by a unipolar world order andafter the disintegration of the Soviet Union, Primakov aimed at enhancing Russia's stand in the world through this initiative. Initially, the idea was unsuccessful, however, in 2003, foreign ministers of the three nations held a trilateral meeting for the first time. Further independent meetings have been held since 2005 transforming the RIC into a diplomatic brand. Therefore, in the Russian discourse, the RIC is regarded as a dialogue mechanism between the three nations rather than as a strategic trianglebecause till now the arrangement has not been used to address any common set of objectives (Denisov, 2017).

The Primakov Doctrine marked a shift in Russian Foreign policy from a Westernist to a Statist school of thought.Westernists recognize the West as an advanced civilization and instead of being in conflict, Russia should rather follow it. Statists, on the other hand, believe that Russia should be a strong independent power capable of ensuring safety both from the West and East. In the 1990s, the Westernist school of thought in Russian foreign policy lost prominence. In 1996, Andrei Kozyrev, a westernist was replaced by Primakov, a statist as Minister of Foreign Affairs. The Primakov Doctrine is essentially a foreign policy approach that seeks a balance of power and multipolarity. As per the doctrine, instead of competing with the USA alone, Russia should align with other major powers to position itself as an indispensable state whose consent is necessary for any major issue faced by the international community. An argument formultipolarity was also made according to which a multipolar world will ensure checks and balances on any unilateral use of power. The Primakov Doctrine has three major components. First is Russian primacy in the post-Cold War era marked by close and strong relations with former Soviet states. The second is opposing the eastward expansion of NATO with constant efforts to weaken the US-led world order. The third component is a partnership with China(Rumer, 2019).

Newly formed Russia held the view that in the post-Cold War era, USA and Russia would be cooperating in world affairs. Instead, Russia faced disappointments on multiple occasions over the years. A large amount of economic assistance from the USA that Russia expected was not met. In 1991, the Warsaw Pact was disbanded and Russia expected the same for NATO. Instead, NATO continued to exist with further eastward expansion toward former Warsaw Pact nations. Russia was also criticized by the USA for its suppression of Chechen rebels in 1999. Further, the USA intervened in Kosovo and Bosnia and conducted bombings in Serbia even though Russia objected to any American intervention in Yugoslavia against Serbia. This led Russia to realize that the USA was taking advantage of theirsoft approach to expand its influence.Therefore, Moscow decided that it must take a standagainst Washington rather than make any further concessions like the 1989 peaceful withdrawal from Eastern Europe and other third-world nations. The American hegemony was opposed by several nations globally which usually included India, China, Iran, Iraq, Syria, Serbia, multiple Commonwealth of Independent States (CIS), and also Germany and France. Since Russia in itself was not strong enough to counterbalance the USA, Primakov hoped that Russia could lead the nations that were against the American hegemony (Katz, 2006). It is in this background that Primakov sought to build a consensus with India and China to counterbalance the USA. At that time, Russia-China relation was moving in the same direction but Moscow held the view that including India in the alliance would increase the appeal of multipolarity and its rule-based liberal democratic ideals would add legitimacy to the alliance (Hsiung, 2019).

An attempt to formally institutionalize the doctrine was made in 1998 when Primakov, proposed cooperation among the three nations during his visit to India. The idea was largely rejected both by China and India as both nations shared valuable trade ties with the USA. Other reasons included the India-China border issues and the perception that the idea was driven more by Russian ambitions against the West rather than a genuine stride toward cooperation and multipolarity (Hsiung, 2019).India's decision not to affirm the idea was influenced by multiple factors. India at the time did not want to deflect from its non-alignment posture and was concerned that welcoming such an idea would include India into an overt anti-American coalition. India also had reservations regarding sharing a platform with China due to its direct support to Pakistan in Kashmir and continued tensions at the border (Lo, 2017). Due to this, the Primakov Doctrine lapsed and Russia shifted its priorities towards strengthening its bilateral ties with China.

While the original idea of the alliance was ineffective, multiple catalysts led to a revival of the idea. The 2008 financial crisis put the US-led financial system under scrutiny. In response, alternatives to the existing financial order were considered making a non-Western coalition more plausible. Later, between 2011-2012, anti-Putin protests erupted in Russia. The blame was put on the USA for attempting a regime change. In response, Vladimir Putin wrote an article titled 'Russia and the Changing World' which emphasized the role of India and China in the international community. Further, the imposition of Western sanctions upon the Russian annexation of Crimea in 2014 created additional imperatives for pursuing such an alliance (Lo, 2017). All these developments renewed attention to Russia-India-China strategic alliance and put the Primakov Doctrine back on the Russian foreign policy agenda.

Since the RIC in order to function would require cooperation on a larger scale, it is likely that the border dispute would not allow a conducive environment for cooperation. However, India and China are already members of other multilateral platforms along with Russia like the BRICS which constitutes of Brazil, Russia, India, China, and South Africa, and the Shanghai Cooperation Organisation (SCO) which includes Russia, India, and China along with Iran, Pakistan, Tajikistan, Uzbekistan, Kyrgyzstan, and Kazakhstan. These two organisations have been deemed successful institutions that are non-western and have provided a counterbalance to the Western order in the international political system. Therefore, India and China have already been cooperating on multilateral platforms despite their border issues. Further, in the case of ASEAN, the member states have been able to foster cooperation despite multiple bilateral disputes over territorial claims. Although the RIC has been limited in its successes, it is seen as a precursor to the BRICS and SCO. Considering that states are able to cooperate in a multilateral setting even if bilateral disputes over territorial claims exist, like the member states of ASEAN, India, and China can also cooperate given that there is a convergence of interests and that it would be beneficial to both the countries on a larger scale. The relevance of the RIC in the contemporary era can be justified by the successes of other multilateral platforms like BRICS and SCO since the RIC is said to be the core of both these platforms (Purushothaman, 2018).

In order to transform the current RIC into a strategic alliance, Russia, India, and China will have to address and pursue a common vision.Since the purpose of the Primakov Doctrine was to act as a counterbalance to the US and its allies, the RIC can cooperate on the creation of a monetary framework based on a common currency. This way, providing an alternative to the current financial system, the

RIC could expand its role and objectives which till now have been limited to discussions.

After the Russian invasion of Ukraine, Russia was hit by economic sanctions from the West. After Russian banks were removed from SWIFT, Russia put forward the initiative to create its own version of SWIFT. This initiative is likely to get attention from other nations who either seek an alternative to the US-dominated financial system or are under economic sanctions from the West. These circumstances further create opportunities for other powers like India and China to join Russia in the initiative for creating an alternative financial system.If the RIC, institutionalizes itself as a platform for economic cooperation, it can together achieve these objectives of formulating a new non-western economic structure. However, such cooperation between three nations that have completely different approachesto foreign policy, internal affairs, and economic and political philosophy will be met with a number of challenges like converging the national policiesof each country and establishment of required institutions. Most importantly, the RIC will possibly be perceived as a coalition that goes against the interests of the West. Further, it would also complicate India's role in the Quad which seeks to contain China's influence in the Indo-Pacific. However, if Russia, India, and China are able to foster cooperation despite territorial disputes like ASEAN, the challenges will be outweighed by what it will achieve in the longer run.

The current RIC mechanism – Limitations and Scope:

The 14th RIC foreign ministers' meeting was held on 18 April 2016 in Moscow. The three countries called for a regional security and cooperation architecture that would be open, inclusive, indivisible, and based on universally recognized principles of international law. The meeting led to a trilateral consensus on the need for further cooperation and building security architecture for the Asia-Pacific. However, to achieve the said goals, the RIC would require close cooperation on top-level design and policy planning (Shuai, 2016).So far, the RIC communiques have only mentioned statements regarding commitment to UN and international law, condemning international terrorism, and narcotics, and expressing concern on conflicts around the world. Such statements are not unique and are similar to the declaration of BRICS summits. As a result, the utility of RIC is being questioned by Russian observers. Due to this, President Putin himself suggested that the main value of the RIC is as a building block for BRICS(Lo, 2017).

Four major factors have contributed as impediments to gaining momentum for the RIC. First, Russia, India, and China have completely different political systems whichremain the biggest barrier to the further development of their trilateral ties. Second, there is a divergence of opinion among the public and elites which further hinders any cooperation among the trilateral. For Russia, the RIC is a geopolitical tool for counterbalancing the West, not a grand strategy. On the other hand, India holds a cautious attitude towards the RIC due to its utilitarian principle and sensitivity to the American perception of India having a closer relationship with Russia and China. Third, security concerns and disputes become obstacles to any cooperation in the RIC. Finally, the RIC will have to solve issues at the operational level, trust deficit, and weak cooperation in non-political domains. Non-political issues like economic and people-to-people exchanges are limited due to huge differences in language, religious beliefs, cultural traditions, etc. Due to the absence of deep cultural and people-to-people exchanges, the RIC lacks mutual understanding and therefore remains vulnerable to the changes in world politics (Shuai, 2016).

a. Addressing the India-China dispute:

One of the most important factors that hinder the transformation of the RIC from a dialogue mechanism into a strategic alliance is the strained India-China relationship. Therefore, the very first initiative that the three nations must undertake is to address and resolve the border disputes between India and China.

Since both nations have mistrust over each other's intentions, it has created a perception problem. On the Indian side, the perception is that China is insensitive and indifferent to India's core concerns, while the Chinese perceive that India does not reciprocate China's goodwill. There is a further mismatch of identity perception as well. China does not identify India as a threat and therefore thinks that it is adopting a benign attitude towards India. India on the other hand believes that China does not give an appropriate status to India as a regional power. Unlike China, India does not have any rivalry with the USA nor does it have the global ambition to dominate the world. Hence, China has more to lose from the dispute. China must consider this and give due consideration to India as a major regional power. This would be beneficial for China as well since an antagonistic India will only complicate China's rise in a global political landscape especially when China is subjected to greater suspicion and resistance from the world. Thus, China must ask itself if the strategic and global dimensions of Indo-China relations are weakened to the point that the bilateral disputes are gaining salience. India should also consider the possibilities of policy adjustments toward China in the changing global dynamics (Gokhale, 2021).

Neither China nor India would gain anything from a conflict in the region. Both nations are deep in economic engagements, managing ethnic nationalism and maintaining the legitimacy of the state.Instead, China and India can foster cooperation on issues of arms control, climate change, trade, and labor laws as common ground to counter the Western countries (Malone & Mukherjee, 2010). On 08 September 2022, the Indian Ministry of External Affairs released a statement informing that India and China reached a consensus to disengage their troops in the area of Gogra-Hotsprings i.e., PP-15 in the 16th round of the India-China Corps Commander Level Meeting in a coordinated manner which is essential for maintaining peace in the border areas (MEA, 2022). In light of further cooperation between India and China, such developments show a possible way forward for the feasibility of the RIC.

The initiative to revive and transform the RIC into an active strategic alliance can be possible due to multiple political rhetorics that are common among the three nations. Russia, India, and China, all support the idea of a multipolar world. All three nations support an enhanced role of the United Nations, have criticized NATO's expansion towards the East, and hold an uncompromising position regarding violations of national sovereignty as their own territorial integrity has been challenged in Chechnya, Kashmir, and Taiwan (Kuchins). The Eurasia landmass has been witnessing challenges both in traditional and non-traditional security aspects. In this regard, the RIC can serve as a platform to address the security challenges in the regional landscape. Since, Russia, China, and India are culturally and politically different from each other, there exists no pattern of a single political ideology among the three nations. Therefore, RIC as an alliance would be based solely to fulfil its own strategic interests(Shuai, 2016).

The changes in the global political system can further contribute to the strengthening of the RIC. While emerging powers such as the member nations of the BRICS, experience economic difficulties, the shift of power from Western nations to the East as a trend allows the RIC to create and promote platforms alongside emerging powers ordeveloping states like the BRICS and SCO.

b. Cooperation with existing disputes – the case of ASEAN:

In the case of ASEAN, the Philippine-Malaysia dispute over Sabah made the founding members realize the need for cooperation and resolution of disputes. In the later years, several bilateral maritime disputes emerged like the South China Sea, the Sulu Seas, the Gulf of Thailand, and other regions. However, ASEAN has been able to function successfully despite the disputes. Other issues like Malaysia–Indonesia dispute over the Sipadan and Ligitan Islands in the Sulawesi Sea and Singapore–Malaysiadispute over the Pedra Branca islands in the South China Sea were resolved through arbitration by the International Court of Justice (ICJ). The willingness to bring in an outside body rather than violent confrontation showcases the commitment of ASEAN towards peace and cooperation. During the Cambodian conflict, Neither Vietnam nor Cambodia was an ASEAN member. However, ASEAN negotiated a settlement, while garnering support against the Vietnameseoccupation of Cambodia. Here, it must be noted that while the agreement is called the "Paris Peace Agreement", no Western nation was involved in the settlement process and the real foundations of the agreement were laid in Bogor and Jakarta.

However, issues and disputes within the ASEAN still exist today. Earlier, ASEAN's Secretary-General stated that unresolved issues regarding territorial and maritime claims remain the biggest challenge for ASEAN. Further, the land dispute between Cambodia and Thailand which has led to military standoffs is also a serious challenge to ASEAN's commitment to being a security community. Domestic political factors also become a challenge to ASEAN as was evident in the Thailand-Cambodia conflict. Further, a variety of issues need to be settledlike Singapore's access to Malaysian water andallegations of Malaysian airspace being violated by planes of Singapore's air force.Singapore and Indonesia landed an agreement on the western maritime boundary but are facing problems over extradition. TheSipadan–Ligitan island dispute, an ICJ-mandated settlement has also been disrupted by a new issue between Singaporeand Malaysia over the claim on Ambalat by Malaysia. In the Pedra Brancadispute, the ICJsettlement recognized Singapore's sovereignty over Pedra Branca, but the Middle Rocks which are just adjacent were awarded to Malaysia. So, it can also be a possible source of friction between Singapore and Malaysia (Acharya, 2013).

The ASEAN Political-Security Community Blueprint mentions Confidence Building Measures and Preventive Diplomacy as important tools of conflict prevention that prevent disputes and tensions that arise among the ASEAN Member States and assist in preventing existing disputes to escalate. The actions included under such measures are regional exchanges among military officials including military academies, defense universities, and staff colleges being organized in the ASEAN Member States, observers of military exercises being exchanged and commensurate with the capabilities of all ASEAN Member States, information regarding the submissions to the UN Register of Conventional Arms being shared, promoting exchanges and visits between defense officials and military training institutions to build trust and mutual understanding, and joint research projects government-affiliated policy institutes and strategic research institutes on defense issues. ASEAN has also promoted the Treaty of Amity and Co-operation in Southeast Asia (TAC), according to which the Member States must refrain from the use or threat of force. The TAC provides a provision for the settlement of disputes through friendly negotiations rather than through threats and the use of force. The blueprint suggests strategies meant for the prevention of disputes arising from within ASEAN. This comprehensive approach by ASEAN suggests an understanding among the Member States regarding the settlement of differences or disputes being regulated by rational, effective, and flexible procedures and by refraining from negative attitudes (ASEAN, 2009).

In ASEAN, we see multiple nations who despite their bilateral territorial disputes have been able to manage and function as an organization. This has only been possible as the member nations had a firm realization regarding the need for cooperation on a larger scale to ensure peace, prosperity, and stability. Therefore, while India and China have their own territorial disputes at the border, that does not suggest that they cannot function together on a larger platform.

c. RIC cooperation in BRICS and SCO

RIC must avoid being confined to a strict trio mechanism and cooperation should happen in a broad context. The three nations already cooperate in other multilateral forums. BRICS and SCO are two of the most important such institutionsas they both aspire to create an alternative to Western-led institutions (Hsiung, 2019). Although RIC in itself has not been a functioning platform, its value as a precursor to the BRICS is recognized. BRICS unlike the RIC has also been able to further develop through initiatives like the Contingency Reserve Arrangement and the New Development Bank. In 2018, Russia ranked sixth, India ranked third, and China ranked first in terms of GDP. In the same year, Russia, China, and India ranked second, third and fourth respectively in terms of military power. It was their similar growth rates that paved the way for the formation of the BRICS in 2009 (Bratersky & Kutyrev, 2019).

The most important step toward the institutionalization of the BRICS was the establishment of the New Development Bank (NDB). The NDB provided funding for infrastructure development and shared equal voting rights between all five member nations. Unlike the Western-led financial institutions, the NDB ensured access to loans by developing nations without a rigid process. Thus, BRICS showcased an unexpected success in terms of a new form of global governance and cooperation(Bratersky & Kutyrev, 2019).

The SCO was established with the priority of ensuring security, however, economic cooperation emerged as an objective in the mid-2000s. In 2003, SCO started a program of economic cooperation and multilateral trade. This program initiated over 100 collaborative projects on trade, transportation, finance, energy, and agriculture with the creation of the SCO Interbank Association and the SCO Business Council in consecutive years. Due to the interlinked nature of security and economy, SCO focuses on large-scale infrastructure development projects. The Central Asian region is economically less developed and therefore requires investment for infrastructure development. On the other hand, microeconomic projects are negligible due to concerns that other member nations' economies would not be able to compete with China on the economic front (Aris, 2013).

BRICS focuses on cooperation on non-traditional security challenges while the SCO focuses on traditional security aspects. As Russia, India, and China are a member of both these significant organisations, cooperation in both these platforms covers a broad range of international security issues that are relevant in the emerging multipolar world. Through this, the RIC can further strengthen the discourse for an increased role of non-Western nations in global governance (Shuai, 2016).

Creating a common currency framework

One major objective that can transform the RIC into a strategic alliance is cooperating on an economic architecture based on a common currency. After the Russian invasion of Ukraine in 2022, India and China were among the multiple nations that took a neutral stand on the issue. India which has strong bilateral ties with the USA was severely criticized. This decision showcased India's willingness to go against the Western narratives and keep its historical bilateral ties with Russia primary. In response to the restriction of Russian banks from SWIFT, Russia is taking strides to establish its own financial system. While China is already affirmed with the Russian initiative, India is also seen as a potential partner for the same(Liu, 2022).

The primary benefits of a common currency are that it increases price transparency eliminating the difficulty of price comparison in different countries and eliminating the cost of currency conversions. Further, common currencies also encourage inward investment. In the case of the Euro, a large number of consumers in a single market and the Euro being one of the most significant currencies in the world increased the possibility of investmentsin Europe. One of the major problems in trading with different currencies is the uncertainty of exchange rates which hinders trade, particularly affecting the smaller firms. A single currency zone eliminates this uncertainty encouraging trade within the zone. Establishing a common currency also has its difficulties. Transitioning into a common currency requires short-term costs and executing such a framework requires a single monetary policy with interest rates set for all member countries. There is also a possibility that a single policy will incur differing effects on different countries. A possible roadmap for creating this common currency framework can be found in the Theory of Optimum Currency Areas.

a. Optimum Currency Areas

The Theory of Optimum Currency Areas (OCA) was set forth by Robert Mundell in an article named "A Theory of Optimum Currency Areas," published in 1961. In the article, Mundell raised the question of what economic criteria can lead multiple regions of the world to adopt a common currency. Mundell using North America as an example questioned the circumstances under which Western Canada and

Western USA can create a Western currency or the Eastern parts of Canada and USA can create a common currency only for the East of the continent. This common currency would be governed by a floating exchange rate replacing the Canadian and US dollar.

The Euro serves as a primary example of the adoption of a common currency. The Economic and Monetary Union (EMU) came into effect on 1 January 1999 with initially 11 EU member nations as signatories. Currently, 19 out of 27 European Union member nations have adopted the Euro as the official currency, together forming the Eurozone. Other countries outside the EU like Andorra, Kosovo, Monaco, Montenegro, San Marino, and the Vatican also have Euro as their official currency. Additionally, dependent territories like the Dutch and French overseas territories in the Caribbean, the Indian Ocean, and the Pacific are neither EU nor EMU members but have adopted the Euro. This union aims to develop the internal market of Europe, maintain price levels and keep the currency stable (World Data, n.d.).

After the establishment of the EMU and the adoption of a single currency, the trade costs significantly declined and the integration of trade improved the efficiency of firms in areas of member countries. The integration process also allowed firms in the euro area to increase theircompetitiveness internationally by setting upcross-border production structures.Further trade with other advancedeconomies increased at an annual rate of 4% onaverage while intra-euro trade remained at the same level. Later, the trade that occurred among euro members closed the gap with extra-euro trade after a period of adjustment and increased at a higher rate.Exports from the euro area gained a share in the foreign markets in the first three years after the establishment of the EMU, however, in the following decade, the price competitiveness at the global level slowly declined and stabilized at lower levels. Overall, the adoption of a common currency has enhanced aggregate productivity growth.

Another instanceto be considered is a possible common currency for ASEAN. The Asian Financial crisis of 1997 raised two possible situations for the exchange rate problem i.e., a free float or a hard peg. The idea of adopting a common currency by ASEAN emerged in the aftermath of this crisis.In comparison to the EU, ASEAN has favorable factor mobility, relatively high labor as well as capital mobility and ranks high in terms of wage and price flexibility. Further, multiple ASEAN nations havetrade-to-GDP ratios and trade-intensity ratios higher than in Western Europe. Most importantly, the intraregional trade in ASEAN is 25 percent which is already higher in comparison to other currency unions like the Eastern Caribbean Currency Union (about 10 percent), the Western Africa Economic and Monetary Union (about 10 percent), and the Central African Economic and Monetary Community (about 3 percent) (Madhur, 2002).

However, regarding the idea of a common currency, both cases need to be considered. In the case of Europe, a common currency was the result of mutual understanding and cooperation. On the other hand, ASEAN countries have been cooperating without a common currency. Therefore, a common currency, although may not be essential, can be a possible and effective way forward for greater economic cooperation. Further, if Russia, India, and China are able to create such a monetary framework, the reactions from the world would be threefold. First, nations that see such a development in opposition to their monetary system will oppose it. For instance, the USA and the EU. Secondly, countries in the geographic area that could benefit from the single currency will join. Finally, some nations will stay neutral on the issue. In a social context, the alliance will have an identity of a non-western power bloc. In an economic context, the common currency and the common central bank will foster results similar to the Eurozone. In a political context, the alliance would be able to counterbalance the West by providing an alternative to the existing financial system.

In the case of the Euro, supporters of the adoption of a common currency advocated that the removal of risks associated with the exchange rate would eliminate the costs of transactionsand would increase planning security for trade and investment across the border which would boost the Single Market and increase economic welfarethroughmore competition. The Euro, along with a macroeconomic policy that is oriented towards economic stability will expand the stability further in the region. Further, the Euro meant to increase competition in the Euro area along with the elimination of currency devaluation being used as an emergency exit from economic misalignments would allow structural reforms that would enhance competition, domestic productivity, and growth.However, the fact that a common currency would invite other growth effects with the lowered cost of capital and making the financial market more closely integrated was less appreciated. Finally, the common currency was expected to provide the European Union with a significant presence in the international economy (Regling, Deroose, Felke & Kutos, 2010).

b. Challenges in adopting a common currency for the RIC

For the RIC, adopting a common currency framework would prove to be challenging not just regarding perception but further social, economic and political. Russia, India, and China, all have different approaches to conducting their foreign policy, internal affairs, and economic engagements. Therefore, it is necessary for them to set and arrange several political and economic preconditions which are required for a common currency to function.

In the case of ASEAN, several factors act as constraints to the adoption of a common currency in the region. Here, the diversity in levels of economic development is very large. Among ASEAN, the richest country i.e., Singapore, has a per capita income close to 300 times that of Myanmar, the poorest country in the group. Further, in the ASEAN-5 i.e., Singapore, Indonesia, Thailand, Philippines, and Malaysia, Singapore's per capita income is about 40 times that of Indonesia. This level of difference is higher than in the members of the EU and is argued that such diversity could make a common currency difficult to sustain. Further, if the co-movement of relative prices and outputs across nations is not high, then even if the member countries have perfectly equal per capita incomes, conducting a common monetary policy for the union is difficult. On the other hand, a common currency is less difficult even with different per capita incomes across countries but their co-movement following an economic shock is very high. Further, a weak banking system could undermine an exchange rate regime such as a common currency, inadequate mechanisms for reserve pooling for the region, and the absence of required regional institutions could also be constraints to the common currency. Hence, ASEAN may qualify the economic conditions for adopting a common currency, but it is yet to develop the required preconditions at the political level. Therefore, if the RIC agrees on creating a common currency, the three nations will need to arrange for the required preconditions for such cooperation (Madhur, 2002).

In the case of the Euro, the integration process was long viewed as a way for participating nations to expand their economic and political clout. Although the public in Europe has largely been inclined towards the EU as many citizens valued their freedom to live, work, and travel anywhere throughout Europe, tension still exists between those members of the EU who want a closer union and those who in order to protect their national prefer the EU to be kept on a more intergovernmentalfooting. Therefore, some nations in the EU have opted out of certain aspects regarding the integration in the Eurozone and the Schengen area. Additionally, policy preferences of different member countries are often influenced by their varying geographies and histories. For instance, the expansion of the EU towards the East brought many new members who were formerly in the Soviet Bloc during the Cold War which raises concerns regarding the ties of the EU with Russia. It has been questioned whether the further integration of the EU is compatible with its further enlargement. The criticisms go further to the decision-making processes in the EU being very complicated, lacking transparency, and too slow and unwieldy. While the EU welcomes any European country that fulfills the required economic and political criteria for membership, there are concerns among countries that are culturally distinct regarding the implications of EU expansion on the capacities of EU institutions, finances, and its overall identity. Further observations suggest that as the EU expands encompassing a wider range of countries then further economic integration may be unlikely and that creating a common foreign policy would become more problematic (CRS, 2018).

The De-Dollarization Trend

The discussion regarding de-dollarization started in the year 2000. After the default in 1998, Putin stated that the dollar would not yield any benefits and would make the situation worse, and would also hurt the financial sovereignty. Later, in October 2018, Russian Minister of Finance Anton Siluanov and the Chairman of the Board of VTB Bank Andrey Kostin declared the need for bringing economic reforms which essentially meant a policy to separate from the dollar.

The concept of de-dollarization is the reduction of dependency on the dollar as a currency for international settlements. Further, the use of the US dollar being used for both domestic and foreign trade displaces the national currencies from the turnover, therefore, according to the IMF, while the share of the US in the global economy is 25%, its share in the international gold reserves of the countries is around 63 %. Further, in any event, where the price in the stock market is falling, investors buy other assets which increase the exchange rate of the dollar. This leads to an increased price of the dollar, while the price of the Rouble falls (Gribina & Trushkin, 2020).

In the context of challenging the US dollar, the potential contenders are those with growing influence in the global financial system like the Euro or the Renminbi. Here, it must be noted that there are certain flaws in these two currencies. The performance of the Euro has seen stagnation in the past decades. Further, the financial market of Euro-dominated assets does not have the same depth and size as the US dollar-dominated market which limits the Euro's capacity to challenge the dollar globally. Similarly, the Renminbi also lacks the depth and size of the market dominated by the US dollar. Additionally, Renminbi also lacks a flow of free international capital. Therefore, the general understanding remains that no alternative currency holds the same credibility as the US dollar (Liu & Papa, 2022).

a. De-Dollarization initiatives in BRICS

BRICS hold 24 percent of the global GDP and around 16 percent of global trade and its collective economic power is a challenge to the dominance of the US dollar. Therefore, if BRICS moves away from the dollar, its impact would be worldwide (Liu & Papa, 2022).

In the early literature regarding the collective financial operation of BRICS scholars examined the dynamics of the currency. This literature suggests that BRICS generate a shared common narrative regarding reduction in the dominance of the dollar, however, due to different interests and disagreements any further efforts failed. While scholars have acknowledged the deepening of the financial cooperation of BRICS, there is a disagreement regarding the credibility of initiatives by BRICS to change the current global financial system. The formation of the NDB and CRA are examples of collective mobilization of BRICS towards changing the global financial system, but scholars who are critical of the collective mobilization capabilities of BRICS argue that the grouping's heterogeneity in the polity, economy, and ideology, the power asymmetry among members, and absence of vision regarding the world order which appeals to the international order undermines its collective mobilization capabilities. For instance, the failed attempt by BRICS to create its credit rating agency serves as an example of BRICS' limitations for reforming the global financial order. Further, there also exists a dilemma for BRICS where they prefer to have an alternative to the US dollar, but the depreciation of the dollar decreases the value of the holdings of the assets denominated by the dollar (Liu & Papa, 2022).

b. De-Dollarization initiatives from Russia and China

In 2017, the USA under the Trump administration adopted the Countering America's Adversaries Through Sanctions Act (CAATSA). Russian efforts of de-dollarization increased when companies owned by Russian billionaire Oleg Deripaska were put under sanctions by the US. In this regard, President Vladimir Putin criticized the US for weaponizing finance which was reducing the trust in the dollar as an instrument of universal payment and the primary currency reserve. After Russia invaded Ukraine, Kremlin focused more on securing all financial spheres and the plans for de-dollarization were neglected. Unlike 2014, this plan was focused more on switching to rouble-denominated payments whenever it could. Thus, the move away from the dollar became geoeconomically crucial as evident in the recent demand by Russia for switching to the rouble for payments in the trading of gas with Europe.

The war in Ukraine has presented an opportunity for India and China where they could strengthen their partnership with Russia economically and go ahead with creating an alternative financial system. Since, both India and China did not condemn Russia for the war in Ukraine, this could also indicate a possibility of India and China emerging as key partners in the de-dollarization efforts. Before the invasion of Ukraine, Russian banks had limited dealings in Yuan but after the invasion, the Russian banks started using Yuan with great enthusiasm (Shagina, 2022).

China's vision of de-dollarization started with the development of its system called the Cross-Border Interbank Payment System (CIPS). In the year 2020, both Russia and China have reduced their dollar-based exchanges by 50% and could also make other compatible alternative systems to SWIFT. China has been working towards the long process of moving away from the dollar as President Xi Jinping envisions a strong economy and financial relevance for China (Pedraz, 2022).

China has started to use Yuan for its payments for Russian coal with other commodity producers also shifting to Yuan. In this regard, China has not denied the possibility of using Roubles or Yuan for trade in the energy sector with Russia. Such an agreement also existed during the Soviet era when payments were facilitated in national currencies. Russia and India have increased the use of their national currencies for bilateral trade since 2014. As a result, the trade in national currencies between the two countries rose from 6% to 30%. Since the Russian invasion of Ukraine, India and Russia have come up with an alternative platform for transactions that would facilitate trade in rupees and roubles. This new system would be set up between India's Reserve Bank of India (RBI) and Russia's VEB (Shagina, 2022).

Regarding the Russian invasion of Ukraine, there exists a major flaw in the assessments by Western countries. A more accurate assessment comes from Hudson Lockett in an article in the Financial Times which shows the ongoing war in Ukraine as a move that will accelerate the trend of de-dollarization. This trend is a goal for Russia and China while certain actions by the Indian government and the business community suggests a willingness to participate in this trend (Caldararo, 2022).

RIC in the context of Indo-Pacific

In discussions regarding the RIC, India's membership in the Quad cannot be ignored. The revival of the Quad from its nascent stage is attributed to China's growing assertiveness in the Indo-Pacific. Despite the efforts not to project the Quad as an anti-China alliance, its establishment is understood as an attempt to contain the growing Chinese influence. The term Indo-Pacific, unlike Asia-Pacific, recognizes India as a rising power and its role in the balance of power in Asia in the future. Additionally, India's credentials as a democracy and affirmation of rules-based order offer assurance to other Quad nations. Further, the recognition of India's influence and the need for its cooperation to uphold freedom of navigation and overflight is aligned with India's ambitions (Chaudhury & de Estrada, 2018).

While the Quad allows a platform for India to further expand its influence in the Indo-Pacific and counterbalance China in the region, it is also likely to create disadvantageous circumstances for India-China relations as well. The grouping can revamp tensions between India and China which would affect cooperation in other multilateral platforms like the BRICS and SCO. Therefore, it is most favorable to India that the Quad is not reduced to an anti-China alliance. Among the Quad members, India is the only country that shares borders with China and has experienced military standoffs. Therefore, India needs to make sure not to create circumstances that would lead to military aggression between the two countries (Pant, 2022).

India's commitment to the RIC can be viewed as a breakaway from the Quad. However, the economic cooperation in the RIC will only be a component of its multi-alignment approachto create an alternative financial system.The monetary framework of a common currency would be limited to purely economic grounds and will have no overlapping of interests with the Quad initiatives in the Indo-Pacific. Therefore, to avoid any complications in this context, the RIC will have to be very careful regarding its perception.

Policy Recommendation

In order to transform the RIC into an effective platform of economic cooperation, multiple policies need to be enacted.

- Firstly, it must be noted that India and China are partners in trade and have been able to keep their economic engagements intact despite the issue. Here, both India and China need to realize the importance of cooperation on larger issues. Lessons can be drawn from other multilateral forums like the BRICS and SCO where India and China gave already been cooperating on a larger scale. For this, greater economic cooperation through the RIC can be used as an incentive to avoid any further military standoffs.
- Second, the idea of the trilateral was a failure since both India and China were particular about not appearing to join a coalition that is anti-West. Further, India's membership in the Quad and its vision of ensuring a free and open Indo-Pacific can also act as a hurdle to the RIC as the Quad is largely seen as a coalition to contain China in the region. This is a concern that still exists today. Therefore, it must be made clear that the RIC is an economic forum and has no overlapping with other initiatives in the region. For this, communication at the political level needs to be very clear about the monetary framework to avoid any misperception.
- Third, Russia, India and China will have to reach the necessary preconditions required for a common currency. These preconditions are economic, political, social and institutional. Therefore, the three nations will have to ensure that the political rhetoric and favour of the people are aligned with the integration along with the creation of the institutions necessary for economic integration.
- Fourth, the adoption of a common currency needs to happen gradually through a series of policy initiatives. In the case of the Euro, the member states ensured free movement of capital among member states,

followed by converging economic policies and cooperation between the central banks of the member countries, and then implemented the common monetary policy. For instance, theEMU was created in response to economic instability at the macro level. With the foundation of the EU, the member nations were set forward for creating a "common market" for trade. Later it became apparent that closer economic cooperation was needed for the European economy todevelop which led to active steps toward ensuring economic stability at the macro-level and avoiding disruptions to theSingle Market. Finally, the monetary integration in Europe with a single currency was enshrined in the Maastricht Treaty of 1992.

- Finally, the RIC in its current stage has only seen success regarding the creation of other platforms like the BRICS and SCO which have been successful non-Western multilateral institutions. Here, the RIC can further extend its cooperation on economic agendas on a much larger scale beyond Russia, India, and China if it aligns its objective with platforms like the BRICS and the SCO.

Conclusion

When Yevgeni Primakov proposed the idea of a strategic trilateral consisting of India, China, and Russia, he envisioned a coalition consisting of non-western allies led by Russia to counterbalance the influence of the USA in global affairs. At the time, factors like the India-China dispute and relations with the West led to its failure. Presently, although the three countries still meet on a regular basis, it has been limited to a discussion group and is credited with being the precursor to successful non-Western platforms like the BRICS and SCO. This indicates that India and China despite their border disputes are already cooperating on a larger scale. However, the transformation of the RIC into a platform for economic cooperation would require greater cooperation among the three countries.

The choice of the means of payment in cross-border transactions had been a priority in international monetary architecture in the past. However, after the Bretton Woods Regime collapsed in the early 1970s, it got a non-priority status. When President Richard Nixon announced the end of the dollar's convertibility into gold, a new global monetary framework was made in which private banks could make international payments in the national currencies of the so-called 'strong' currency countries instead of gold exchanges by central banks. With this decision, the value of the US dollar was allowed to float i.e, its value is determined by the shifts in the demand and supply of the currency. There has been an assumption that the euro with increasing its shares in the international system, will continue the ongoing strong-currency regime, however, Europe is unlikely to continue that trend. If no other country or region takes change to provide the other countries to earn a preferred reserve currency, a national currency-based international monetary system will cease to continue. With the dollar being the key currency, countries with well-developed markets were able to promote growth and maintain liquidity. However, the less developed market has experienced shocks similar to the experiences under the gold standard and through the Second World War. Upon the invasion of Ukraine by Russia and the sanctions that are being put on Russia, there exists an opportunity to balance the world order if the RIC cooperates on creating an alternative financial system. This way, the RIC could function as a platform for economic cooperation.

It must be noted that factors that led to the failure of the Primakov Doctrine in the first place still exist today, especially the India-China border dispute. Among the RIC, Russia enjoys cordial relations with both China and India. However, tense relations between India and China are perhaps the biggest obstacle to a successful RIC. As of now, the negotiations between India and China regarding their border dispute at the LAC have largely been at a standstill. Further, China's expansionist approach and intrusion add to the mistrust India has regarding China. These mistrusts have led to complicated India-China relations. A successful RIC would require greater cooperation between India and China since the existing mistrust and disputes only negate the feasibility of the RIC as an efficient platform. Therefore, it is important that the benefits of cooperating with China on a larger scaleare discussed in negotiations and the economic benefits are incentivized for cooperation.

India and China have already been cooperating in BRICS and SCO and a monetary framework based on a common currency will act as an objective that the RIC can pursue as a trilateral.Since an initiative of this kind is likely to create a perception of it being an anti-West coalition, therefore, it is crucial that the RIC has no overlapping interests with other initiatives.

References

Acharya, A. (2013). *ASEAN 2030: CHhallenges and Building a Mature Political and Security Community.* Retrieved from Asian Development Bank Institute: https://www.adb.org/sites/default/files/publication/156296/adbi-wp441.pdf

Archick, Kristin (2018). The *European Union: Ongoing Challenges a*nd Future Prospects, CSR Report No. R 44249 dt Dec 3, 2018. Retrieved from: https://crsreports.congress.gov/product/pdf/R/R44249

Aris, S. (2013, Decembe*r). Mapping Multilateralism in Transition. Re*trieved from International Peace Institute: https://www.ipinst.org/wp-content/uploads/publications/ipi_e_pub_shanghai_cooperation.pdf

ASEAN. (2009). ASEAN Political-Security Community *Blueprint. Retrie*ved from ASEAN: https://asean.org/wp-content/uploads/2021/03/APSC_BluePrint.pdf

Bratersky, M., & Kutyrev, *G. (*2019). BRICS and the Evolving Russia-India-China Security Agenda. Strategic An*alysis.*

*Caldararo, N. L. (2022). Putin, China, In*vasions in Europe and De-Dollarization: Fighting a Longer War. SSRN.

Denisov, I. (2017). Rus*sia-India-China Triangle - From Russian Perspective. 11th Berlin* Conference on Asian Security (BCAS) . German Institute for International and Security Affairs.

Dongxiao, C., & Shuai, F. (2016). The Russia-India-China Trio in the Changing International System. Retrieved from World Scientific: https://www.google.com/url?sa=t&rct=-j&q=&esrc=s&source=web&cd=&cad=rja&uact=8&ved=2ahUKEwj3r*8L-g26z5AhVch-YKHc02BtwQFnoECAQQAQ&url=*https%3A%2F%2Fwww.worldscientific.com%2Fdoi%2Fpdf%2F10.1142%2FS2377740016500275&us-g=AOvVaw3HDVG0Q5SM8jvExt4sKJS8

Estrada, K. S., & Chaud*hury, R. R. (2018). India, the Indo-Pacific and the Quad.* Retrieved from Researchgate: https://www.researchgate.net/publication/325490836_India_the_Indo-Pacific_and_the_Quad

George, Jordana (n.d.). Members of the EMU: Econ*omic and Monetary Union, World data: https://www.worlddata.info/trade-agreements/em*u-economic-and-monetary-union.php

Gokhale, V. (2021). The Road from Galwan: The Future of India-China Relations. Retr*ieved from Carnegie I*ndia: https://carnegieindia.org/2021/03/10/road-from-galwan-future-of-india-china-relations-pub-84019

Gribina, E., & Trushkin, G. (2020). Dedolarization as an indicator of the Formation of National-Oriented Public Policy. Retrieved from Atl*antic P*ress: https://www.atlantis-press.com/proceedings/iscfec-20/125936575

Hsiung, C. W. *(2019). A tenuous trilateral? Retrieved from Swedish Insti*tute of International Aff*airs: https://www.ui.se/globalassets/ui.se-eng/publications/ui-publications/2019/ui-brief-no.-1-*2019.pdf

Kate Sullivan de Estrada, R. R.-C. (2018). India, the Indo-Pacific and the Quad. Survival.

Katz, M. N. (2006). *Primakov Redux? Putin's Pursuit of "Multipolarism"* in Asia. Demokratizatsiya The Journal of Post Soviet Democratization.

Kuchins, A. C. (n.d.). Russia's Relations with China and India: Strategic Partnerships, Yes; Strategic Alliance*s, No. Retrieved from Demokratizatsiya: https://demokratiza*tsiya.pub/archives/09-2_Kuchins.PDF

Liu, Z. Z., & Papa, M. (2022). Can BRICS De-dollarize the Global Financial System? Retrieved from Cambridge University Press: https://www.cambridge.org/core/elemen*ts/can-brics-dedollarize-the-global-financial-sys*tem/0AEF98D-2F232072409E9556620AE09B0

Lo, B. (2017). New Order for Old Triangles? The Russia-China-India Matrix. Retrieved from French In*stitute of Internation*al Relations: https://www.ifri.org/en/publications/notes-de-lifri/russieneivisions/new-order-old-triangles-russia-china-india-matrix

Madhur, S. (2002). Costs and Benefits of a Common Currency for ASEAN. Retr*ieved fr*om Asian Development Bank: https*://www.adb.org/sites/default/files/publication/28307/wp012.pdf*

MEA. (2022, September 08). Disengagement at PP-15. Retrieved from Minsitry of External Affairs, India: https://www.mea.gov.in/press-releases.htm?dtl/35688/Disengagement+*at+PP15*

*Mukherjee, R., & Mal*one, D. (2010). India and China: Conflict and Cooperation. Survival.

Pant, H. V. (2022, March 18). India and the Quad: Chinese belligerence and Indian resilience. Retrieved from Melbo*urne Asia Review: https://melbourneasiareview.edu.*au/india-and-the-quad-chinese-belligerence-and-indian-resilience/?print=pdf

Pedraz, B. R. (2022). Economic War against Russia. Retrieved from Spanish Institute for Strategic Studies: https://www.ieee.*es/Galerias/fichero/docs_opinion/2022/DIEEEO58_2022_BELROM_Rusia_ENG.pdf*

Purushothaman, U. (2018, December). Why RIC is as important to India as JAI and BRICS. Retrieved from Observer Research Foundation: https://www.orfonline.org/ex*pert-speak/why-ric-is-as-impor*tant-to-india-as-jai-and-brics-46213/

Regling, K., Deroose, S., Felke, R., & Kutos, P. (2010). The Euro After Its First Decade: Weathering the Financial Storm and Enlarging the *Euro Area. Retrieved from Asian Development Bank Institute: https:*//www.adb.org/sites/default/files/publication/156060/adbi-wp205.pdf

Rumer, E. (2019). The Primakov (Not Gerasimov). Retrieved from Carnegie Endowment for International Peace: https://carnegieendowment.org/2019/06/05/primakov-not-gerasimov-doctrine-in-action-pub-79254

Shagina, M. (2022, May). Western Financial Warfare and Russia's De-Dollarization Strategy. Retrieved from Finnish Institute of International Affairs: https://www.fiia.fi/wp-content/uploads/2022/05/bp339_western-financial-warfare-and-russias-de-dollarization-strategy.pdf

Index

D

E

F

G

H

N

O

P

Q

R

S

T

U

V

W